Walking Soulfully

By Gary German

WALKING SOULFULLY

Copyright Gary German, 2020

All rights reserved. Except for brief passages quoted in newspaper, magazine, radio, television or online reviews, no portion of this book may be reproduced, distributed, or transmitted in any form by any means, electronic or mechanical, including photocopying, recording, or information storage or retrieval system, without the prior written permission of the author.

ISBN 978-0-578-73667-9

Manufactured in the United States of America
First printing October 2020

Acknowledgments

In gratitude to White Eagle, the Ascended Masters, and the muses who awakened me during the night instructing me to writing. In gratitude to those who persisted when I was resistant.

In gratitude to those who stood by me during many hours of prayer.

Table of Contents

Foreword	i
Introduction	1
Chapter 1: The Soul's Journey	7
My Birthday	7
You Are a Sanctuary of the Soul	14
We Experience the Soul Through the Virtues	17
The Soul Connects Us to Everything	18
The Spiritual and the Tangible	19
Father Paul's Wisdom	21
True Remembering	23
The Soul Reveals Itself	24
The Soul is the Imagination Reflecting	26
Bringing It Down to Earth	27
How Do You Experience the Soul?	29
The Experience of Awe	30
Mythology and Soul	31
Relating with the Soul	32
What is Synchronicity?	32
An Early Morning Meditation	34
Living Soulfully	38
Living a Soulful Life in the World	40
Walking Soulfully	41
What are Soul Moments?	42
Making Choices	44
What Is and Intention?	46
What Does it Mean to Have a Practice?	47
Doing the Work: Being Ready	48
Choices, Identity, and Persona	50
Unhealthy Personas	63

Rekindling a Connection with the Soul   68

Chapter 2: Spiritual Presence   75
What is Spiritual Presence?   78
Presence as Invitation   79
The Practice of Presence   80
The Journey of the Soul   81
Bringing It Deeper Through Meditation   82
Stepping Out of Chaos into Peace   86
Calming Emotions   90
Taming Entities   91
Purity vs Impurity   92
Adding Presence to Your Daily Life   96
Presence and Intention   99
Presence and the Imagination   100
The Dark Imagination   106
From Darkness to Light   108
Getting in Touch with Peace   110
Increasing the Light   110
Spiritual Nourishment   112
Compassion and Service   113
A review: What Is Spiritual Presence   114
An Encouragement   118
Ways to Practice Spiritual Presence   119

Chapter 3: The Alchemy of Soul   121
What is Alchemy, and How it applies to Our Lives?   121
The Law of Interdependence   123
The Matrix of the Soul   124
A Journey Into the Highest Light   126
The Soul is Holographic   127
Paradigms   128
Liminality   129
Soul Messages from a Lakota Symbol   132

Practical Alchemy	133
Redirecting Spiritual Energy	134
Creating a Stupa	135
The Spirituality of the Stupa	138
Rising Above It	139
Beyond Time and Space	140
Transformative Growth	141
Biodiversity	143
Compassion, a Quantum Leap	144
Spiritual Alchemy	145
Transformation and Meditation	146
About that Color Blue	147
Love is Alchemy	148
A Powerful Forgiveness Exercise	150
The Peacock and the Road Runner	151
Alchemy is All about Change and Growth	152
Alchemy and the Body	153
Seeds of Wisdom	154
How Alchemy Unfolds in my Daily Life and Prayer	156
The Master Visits	157
The Theory of Relativity	159
Seeds to Ponder	162
Chapter 4: The Soul and Abundance	**165**
What Does Having Abundance Mean for You?	165
The Realization of Abundance	166
What is Abundance?	167
The Saboteur	168
The Higher Power	170
Aligning Yourself with Your True Calling	170
Consciousness and Abundance	171
The Source	177
Chinguetti	179
The Saints	181

Harmony and Peace	181
The Soul and Financial Concerns	184
Spiritual Abundance	186
Summary Questions: Thoughts to Ponder	
Abundance as a Spiritual Process	189

Suggested Readings   **195**

Foreword

This book may lead you on the journey to your authentic self. For some people, it will help you be aware of your true identity and offer the means to step into that journey. We are always brushing up with or even against our authentic selves, therefore, learning when and how we are doing that is vital for spiritual growth and happiness. Your spiritual growth and happiness matters. The key is the soul. When we identify with what the soul is, its purpose, and how to work with and through it we literally have the keys to ours and others happiness. In this book I challenge current definitions of the soul and demonstrate ways to connect to it.

This book arises from deep spiritual reflection and a desire to share my passion about the soul. I am writing a message about the soul because of a great need in the times. I believe that the soul is what many of us are looking for. The soul is a guiding principle for those seeking a spiritual connection, for those who want to make sense of life. It is always present for those who are searching. There are many who are on a quest and feel guided by the soul. As a collective entity, the soul involves everyone and all life forms on the planet. We are intimately in tune with all that exists, with all other humans and all of life. At the same time, all that exists is in tune with us, even knows us. This book is meant to help people get in touch with the ubiquitous nature of the soul and gives instruction for how to know the essence of the soul.

This book comes from lived experience, a deep curiosity to learn, and from diligent study culminating in the completion of two master's degrees and a doctoral degree. My life reflections were shaped from having crossed cultures, and also from having grown up on a farm in rural Nebraska where I was surrounded by nature.

At age twenty-two I entered seminary life for training to become a Franciscan priest. Seminary life and training brought me through many experiences. I lived in areas of diversity and poverty in the cities of Indianapolis and Chicago. As part of theology training, I lived for five months on the Oglala, Lakota Reservation in South Dakota. That was in 1984. While there, I was invited by the native people and medicine men to participate in the Lakota Sioux rituals. Powerful visions furthered my spiritual growth and life experience, and my life was significantly changed.

When I returned to theology classes my professors and counselors weren't able to relate to my experiences with the Lakota. I spent years between worlds, trying to understand my place in this world. Somehow my world had been opened up to cross-cultural and universal levels. The only thing that made sense to me was that I had an impassioned soul that desired union with the Divine. So, I followed the way of St. Francis of Assisi and community, but inwardly, I was always drawn to the wisdom of other religions as well. I have learned that through the study of other religions I was more readily able to understand the deeper aspects of my own.

Two years after my experience with the Lakota, ministry as a deacon took me to San Antonio, Texas, to work among Latino populations. I lived in the bilingual setting for ten years and spent a year in Mexico. While in Mexico I lived for three weeks among the Huichol Indians in the mountains of Nayarit and through dreams, received communications from a medicine man there. By this time, I had been exposed to a lot of cross-cultural experience and training.

In the spring of 1987, I was approached by a medicine man named, Armando Hernandez, who informed me that he was sent from Arizona to find me. Armando helped me acclimate to a universal understanding through love and wisdom. This began a relationship that placed me on, both physical and spiritual journeys with much learning. Armando and I spent at least three to six hours together every week while I lived in South Texas. He became a good friend and a man of great wisdom.

Armando prepared me for the changes that are now upon us. Most of what he talked about is currently happening. But much of my time with him was an instruction about the soul. Armando was not my only teacher, as I knew several medicine men of good rapport who loved teaching, and other non-Native teachers happened along the way. Their instruction drew me to further study.

After San Antonio, I was stationed among the Laguna and Acoma Pueblo Indian Nations of New Mexico. While with the Pueblo people I was spiritually inspired and challenged. It was a time of intense growth for me. But due to ill health from my trip to the mission lands in Mexico, and with ever pondering questions, I left the priesthood in January 2000. I rested for two years to regain health and strength and accommodate myself to my life's experiences. At the time I was living in Alameda California and began work as a chaplain for a hospice company. The East Bay has as many as 143 different cultures. Hence, many families I ministered to in the East Bay area offered unique experiences.

I met my partner Wilhelm Oosthuizen in June of

2000. Wilhelm is a natural teacher with a very curious mind. He reflects deeply until answers come to his questions. Wil taught me how to reflect, and what to look for while putting together the plethora of life's experiences. Through the influence of his companionship and encouragement and a boost from a wonderful professor and friend, Marilyn Fowler, I became professor of Native American Spirituality and Archetypal Mythology at John F. Kennedy University in California. I also performed workshops for a number of years. Little did I know that being an instructor and teacher could bring so much together for my own wholeness.

Introduction

There is presently great uncertainty on the planet, but unfortunately, I find that few people are prepared for the changes that are upon us. Many structures that we depended on in the past are breaking down. In many cases, what used to be dependable is no longer so. However, given the fact that old structures are breaking down suggests that we are on a new threshold, the threshold of a new beginning. But to get there we need to understand why the old is breaking down. Why are the old structures no longer working for us? Simply put, they are not serving the true needs of humanity, or of the environment we live in anymore.

To support ourselves through this lengthy process of disintegration we need to go beyond the tensions of life and re-attune to the Divine flame, that life within us that supports us. The dawn of a new creation is a daily event. People are seeking advice and wisdom outside of the structures that once provided support. This is a time of significant change. People are asking, what really matters now at this time in my life?

This book addresses some of that question. As stated above, the soul is what many of us are looking for. This book argues that the soul is not an individual thing. We do not have an individual soul; rather, we are all part of The Soul. It is a collective soul that feels to be personal and is indeed very much part of our personal lives. An individual soul is an illusion. We are all connected. If you experience that you are connected to the heart of the Divine, you are part of a universal soul.

Evidence of our collective soul connection is found in

that we are often touched by gestures of other people. Compassion, friendship, love, and joy are infectious and nurture our lives. These are the deep-felt emotions that give us a sense of meaning. We ourselves feel care and compassion for people of other races, religions, and foreign countries. At the very heart of each individual, we know that we are not separated by race, culture or religion. If we hear of someone being ill in another part of the world, we wish them well. Misfortunes are collective experiences. We know this from within ourselves because we are all connected.

We are also deeply disturbed by destructive actions that other people perform. A deep sense within us tells us that corruption and terrorism are wrong. There are responses from countries from all over the world when atrocities happen. Offenses of humanity against humanity and humanity against nature bother us. People in general have concern for the environment. When someone in our neighborhood gets into a brawl or when someone dies of an alcohol or drug overdose, a deep sorrow accompanies us. This is because within we all inherently know that we are deeply connected. All on this planet are experiencing the beginnings of the effects of global warming. As a collective family people are concerned. The consciousness of the collective experience of our unity is rising. We are experiencing the phenomenon of collective concern.

From the mind of soul, we are one people on this planet. What happens to an individual or a country happens to all of us either directly or indirectly. This is evidence of a living collective soul. We are humanity. As human beings we are dependent on one another and upon the environment. There is no escaping it. This writer believes that from the eyes of heaven, we are not just an individual, we are also members of a family, a community, and of humanity. This is evidence of the collective soul. Unless we have rationalized it away, we feel it in our bones. On the collective level we know this. On the spiritual level we are it.

While this book reveals some of my mystical experiences, the contents of my writing is not just for the mystic. I believe it is for many people to read. This book names the attributes and essence of the soul, which are the virtues. The soul, in turn, is an attribute of the Divine. Yet it resides within us and all other beings. In this manner, the soul is a hologram as we are all made of the same Divine light. The essence of the soul is pure Light. It is also intelligence.

With this publication, I offer ways to connect to the soul and its purpose, and to know it as the bringer of peace. The journey of the soul is presented, describing how over the years I have connected the pieces of life into coherency. The Divine aspect of the soul is beyond time and space, but through the soul, Divinity is brought into time and space and resides within us. It is interested in our lives and our growth in consciousness. Being beyond time and space, the soul is infinitely wiser than we are. As a connector to Divinity it balances our lives bringing direction, healing and peace. It can do this because we are made of the same substance of the soul, it is part of the fabric of our being.

As such, you and I are a sanctuary for the soul and what we do with our lives does make a difference. The journey of the soul is about becoming aware of what we already know, that we are interconnected with each other and with all life on this planet and everywhere else where there is life. We are interconnected to every physical and spiritual dimension that exists, known, and unknown. I have learned from my exposure to Native and tribal medicine men that when science learns how to work with this spiritual interconnection humans will have a far-reaching explosion in scientific discovery. As noted above, the keys of living a soulful life are the virtues. Through the virtues we create the divine connection. Through the virtues, we open doorways to understanding the bigger picture, which allows for new creations. What is intended through love and compassion happens.

Connecting with the journey of the soul helps us connect the pieces of life, as they come to us. The soul is like a Divine director showing us the path that works for us in the grander scheme of things as well as in the minutiae of our daily lives. It puts our experiences of life together into a comprehensive whole. Wholeness is perceived by calling upon the awareness principle that is already active within us. Presence and awareness are keys to the soul's wisdom and its workings that are happening in, through and around us. You will experience that the soul always works through and toward peace and harmony. As such, the soul is the bringer of sanity during times of change. In fact, when the soul is activated within, it often uses the imagination to teach us how to be in harmony.

There is an enormous amount of information coming at us in our everyday lives. The world of electronics feeds our imagination from the collective, influencing our choices, telling us what to seek, and believe. But for the individual, too much stimulation away from the imagining that the soul desires for you bogs you down and disrupts your happiness.

While the world of electronics connects us to each other, the soul is the innate connection we have to the

Divine director within us, hence, it connects us to each other and ourselves. Because we are empowered through the soul, we have a need to connect, communicate, and work with it. This means we have a need to live soulfully. One lives soulfully by keeping love or mindfulness in mind. To live soulfully you may want to ponder the following points:

1. To walk soulfully, you need to desire to know who you are. Who are you authentically? To walk soulfully you need to desire to be on the path toward your authentic self. It may take more than half a lifetime to learn who you are authentically.

2. Have you ever considered what your life-path or calling looks like as seen from the perspective of the Divine?

3. How do you learn what your life-path is? It's one thing to know your life-path, but to what depth do you know it? Do you know it just mentally? Do you know it with understanding? Are you willing to know it, or do you already know it in your emotional being as well as intellectually? Some people emotionally feel the calling but do not understand it when it happens experientially or intellectually.

4. To know the above, that is your whole life's journey right there!

5. To walk soulfully is to experience your inner-self and its desired response to the world. This means being conscious of the world you are in without being wrapped up in fleeting desires and dramas.

6. To bring all the above statements about the soul together, throughout this book I refer to my life of experience and study of the Christian, Native American, Buddhist, and Hindu cultures and beliefs. In a small way, I have made a comparative study of these religions.

This study is not all-inclusive by any means. It is merely an individual's reflection from study and life's experiences as expressed through a pondering belief in the collective soul.

Chapter 1
The Soul's Journey

My Birthday

On my sixth birthday, I wanted to have a walk with God because I knew it was a special day. There was a rainstorm the night before, so I put on my boots and coat and refreshed myself with the early morning March air. Following a cow path brought me to a field of clover. But something happened that changed everything. As the morning sunlight bathed the earth before me, I saw that everything was transparent and made of light. Every single plant had an aura, and every plant was aware of all the other plants. They were relating to each other. Even the weeds, brome grass, and trees were relating to the clover, and the clover to them. The translucent plants were moving and singing in the sun but totally aware of my being in their presence. Aura colors of the rainbow surrounded each tiny and large living thing. Every living thing was a being and was moving in synchronous harmony. Some were dancing and some were singing in the light of the crisp morning sun. But the vision took me deeper when I became aware of what they were saying. They were talking about me. Every single plant there was welcoming me, singing to me, and talking about me. I was taken in to their beautiful world.

In the next moment, I woke up lying on my back in that field. A red-tailed hawk was flying above me. I wondered how I ended up on the ground awakening from a deep sleep yet remembering everything. I stood up to watch the beautiful hawk gracing the morning sky.

But something told me, "Look down." Without questioning I looked and there in front of my feet was a red-tailed hawk feather. I picked up the beautiful feather and caressed it. What struck me was that I was not wet. But everything else around me was wet from the nights rain and heavy morning dew. The red-tailed hawk has been with me ever since. At the young age of six, my orientation toward life was altered from a vision.

Something within me is always reaching beyond human intelligence to an intelligence that surpasses what I experience here. I feel it, am aware of it. To my accepted internal longing, this intelligence surpasses time and space and yet brings order to time and space. I refer to this intelligence as the Divine and believe that I, and all of us, have something called the soul so that the Divine can experience itself.

There is always a yearning for my return to this sense of a fully known yet totally other, the Divine. Yet, over time, I have learned that there is nothing to return to because it is always present. Right here, right now, you and I are forever embraced by something that knows us intimately. It knows us intimately because we are made of what it is made of. We, like all the plants in my childhood vision, are composed of Divine intelligence and Light.

I once shared my childhood vision with the medicine man Armando. He gave me an interesting interpretation saying that I had been taken to the land of paradise. He explained that the images I described from my vision are from the upper world and the first level of heaven. "There was a time that we were all in that garden together," he said. "But when some of us got selfish, we were turned away from the garden. From then on, we were given human bodies and have had to struggle to live. Paradise is the place we all pass through when we die. Some of us stay there and some of us go to higher levels of light and being. Surely you recall the Genesis story of the Garden of Eden?"

"I was in Paradise?" I asked.

Armando answered with an affirmative. He added that, "Once you've been to Paradise you know where you are going when you die, and you can help others find that place when they die." Interestingly enough, as a hospice chaplain I counsel ill and dying patients and their families, which is all about this journey of the soul.

One day I had a vision of a symbol. A circle with a black dot in it is an old image of the sun. The symbol in this vision had a yellow-orange circle with a black dot in the center. Surrounding the sun image was a second larger circle which was reddish in color. It was the red color of the red-tailed hawk tail feathers. When I saw that symbol, I heard the words, "This is the symbol of the red-tailed hawk." The sun is the creative principle. This is because it creates life. All living things on this earth are dependent on the sun for nurturance. Without the sun, there is no life. But the color of the tail feathers of the red-tailed hawk surrounds the sun in the symbol. The symbol looks like an eye. This symbol shows the perspective of seeing through the eyes of the hawk.

You might want to ask, what is the gift of the red-tailed hawk? That hawk showed itself to me, as it circled above me. Hawks are known for their incredible vision. Flying above, it can see a vast expanse of land all at once. Can you imagine the beauty from up there? At the same time, the hawk's vision is so fine-tuned and so focused that even from high in the sky it has the ability to see tiny animals. Small rodents are the hawk's nourishment. So the gift of the hawk is to be able to see the whole picture, all of creation before us, and at the same time to see the small things, the particulars that give us life and nourishment. Hawks are also messengers. As beings of flight they are known by Native Americans to bring messages from other worlds. They help us see the bigger picture.

One of the spiritual gifts of the red-tailed hawk symbol is that Hawks as well as Eagles bring souls back to the Creator at the end of life. It is also a symbol of being brought to the Creator while in the meditative state, or of having a gift of seeing. Hawks help us find or focus on the small things when we are caught in the grand scheme of the forest but looking for the nourishment or wisdom that comes from a single tree. Our world is so full of noise and information it is often difficult for us to locate what we really need. Sometimes remembering the basic tasks that we would like to be attentive to slip by.

Having a human body is all about having this ability to focus and have intention so that we can perform well while on planet earth. Yet, we are part of this vast universe and the soul is what connects us from here in the human body to the cosmos. In other words, the soul gives us inner vision or sight to see what we need to see or know at the time. The cosmos is vast, reaching beyond and into infinity. The cosmos itself is a symbolic image of the Divine. From planet Earth, we can only see bits and pieces of this grand universe. It would be too much for us were we to know the full experience of Divinity all at once. We can only handle so much expansion at a time. That's why I collapsed out in that clover field. I was overwhelmed with the experience. The experience, though completely real, was more than

I could handle. One has to be open and ready for such experiences. Only mystics, Buddhas, sadhus, and yogis who have expanded their consciousness have vast experiences of the Divine without collapsing into unconsciousness. Yet, we all experience them, if not in the daytime, we travel through limitless space and time in our sleep. We just don't remember what we see. But it's there.

In truth, we are all living holographically. Our Super Consciousness is fully participating in all the events of the universe at all times. Yet there is only so much that the little part of us can handle. Hence, we have a soul, which like a transistor, portions these energies down, so that we can experience while existing in a body on finite levels. This is the gift of hawk. We participate in the life of the vast reaches of space and yet we are on planet Earth. The soul allows us to experience myopically and macrocosmically. Miraculously, we do this all the time. There is much more to us than we think. This is because we cannot experience it through the faculty of thinking. There are spiritual planes to everything that exists; there are places and things we cannot see. Yet, the spiritual world and this world are both made of the same substance, light. My childhood vision was a spiritual vision. It is a place that, though is always right here, is beyond the temporal world of here and now. That is why I stated above that something within us is always reaching beyond human intelligence to an intelligence that surpasses what we experience.

In actuality, the soul as an orientation towards the Divine, is our essence. It is the stuff that makes us who we are. The soul is complete and whole and invites us to that completion. As we live our lives, we are knowing ourselves and experiencing ourselves and the universe.

The soul is meant to be experienced and known. When I was eighteen, my dad and I were the only two men on the farm. All of my brothers had moved away to college or had jobs in other cities. It was harvest time, and the urgency to complete the job was at hand. The month of November always presents cooler weather with threats of frost and snow or even freezing rain that could hamper or destroy the harvest. If the crops are not harvested, they may be lost. So, the work of the harvest has to continue until it is completed. After more than two months with long hours of work, the harvest was finally finished. The day after, I felt exhausted throughout my body. Yet, a sense of gratefulness overshadowed me because all of that work had been completed.

I sat down on a bale of hay to feel that gratefulness and it became overflowing. Suddenly, I realized that many birds were singing and chatting in a gleeful chorus. A sense that the birds were celebrating the completion of the harvest became apparent to me. Drawn by the beauty of sound, a part of me had merged into elation with the cacophony of the music of the birds. I looked over the land that had been harvested and felt so grateful that many people and beings would be provided for because the harvest was finished. Yet somehow the thoughts running through my mind were not my thoughts. I was reminded that the grain was all safe in storage bins. But soon everything around me changed, and once again I saw that great light flow from all the living things, the trees, grass, and shrubs. This time, I did not faint, but experienced a loving glow from the earth itself. Gratitude filled me. When I finished my work outside, I went indoors and read Psalm Eight, which begins and ends with the exclamation of praise,

"How great is your name, Oh Lord our God, through all the Earth!" (New American Bible) There is tremendous joy and happiness when The Divine and human work together in harmony. That is our calling, and we do this through our connection to the soul.

The soul wants us to know ourselves as whole and happy, meaning that it wants us to experience the physical, material, and spiritual sides of ourselves leading us to completion and happiness. As human beings on planet earth we often feel separate from our completion because of various forms of suffering, including being caught in materialism, illness and duality. When we hold, or tend to, the aspects of life correctly there is no judgment, only presence, and we are free of competition and fear. The soul itself, though an invisible container, serves as a place of refuge, and safety. The soul holds us in place in this complex universe. It distills chaos into order by bringing the entire stimulus that is coming to us in manageable and comprehensible ways. The soul therefore grants sanity, identity and individuality. At the same time, the soul leads us to the experience of community.

All beings have the seed of the soul within them. It is the part of us that is Divinity. The soul is our link to the human community and all other forms of life. Through the soul we are able to partake of our own uniqueness and individuality while at the same time participate in the plethora of experiences that this planet, indeed the universe, offers. It is the arbitrator and vehicle of the mysteries we seek and experience. Said in another way, the soul is an intimate part of us, it is what we may refer to as the higher self. It is that part of us that is intimately connected with the Divine. That is why actively participating in a life with the soul is so important. It is an invisible container through which we experience, explore, and express ourselves. It is the vehicle through which we experience life, the community, and Divinity.

The soul brings us in touch with sacred time and sacred space. We all come from this place called soul. It is collective. It is not "a soul" but is "the soul." We experience it individually because we are in a body and we have an ego that insists that everything is personal. This is because the ego needs to think and feel an existence, so it makes everything about itself. The ego needs to experience to grow. But to know the soul in its authenticity is to know ourselves and remember who we are. The soul reminds us, that though we dwell in linear time and space, we come from the Divine and are made of Divine substance. I go through periods when I have to remind myself of that.

You are a Sanctuary of the Soul

We are in a human body to become a sanctuary for the soul: a house or temple from which the soul can express itself. The soul is pure and operates from that nature. It needs a sanctuary, a pure heart that respects what it needs. It knows where you are coming from and adjusts itself to your needs. It is always accommodating to your needs. If your life takes a spin, becomes very busy, disturbed, has a tragedy, is facing death, is experiencing loneliness or peace, the soul is there for you, adjusting itself to your need of the time. This is homeostasis.

The soul is always communicating with you. As a hologram, it is attached to everything else that exists and to life after death. It is always preparing you for further growth, if you want it. If you ignore the soul, though present, it may remain quiet until you reach for it again. Other times, it will make or create plenty of noise, even cause you injury, to wake you up to what is going on. This is because the soul is in touch with the archetypes which are powers that are indiscriminate in their behavior.

Archetypes are universal patterns that govern the cosmos. These invisible patterns guide us through life. Being that they are formless, archetypes are beyond mental concepts. Being in touch with archetypes, the soul can take you into realms that go far beyond what appears to be human. This is why mystics often find they are unable to describe or define their unfathomable experiences. The soul brings one beyond the rational or logical mind, beyond thought and form, into another intelligence. One is faced with the unknown.

It may be wise and is often necessary to have a guide, spiritual director, a seasoned counselor or depth psychologist while going through a deep soul journey. The growth process is of course both psychological and spiritual, affecting one's life and well-being on this planet and beyond. These worlds are interconnected with the physical world of nature including the human body, psychological aspects of a person, the spiritual, and archetypal. The upper worlds can do without the lower worlds, but the lower worlds cannot exist without the upper influences. The upper levels of spirituality perceive things about the universe through all levels of existence, those above and those below it. But the unconscious person is not aware of these many realities. Only sometimes are humans given glimpses of these vast levels of interchange. Hence, one does well to pray for wisdom and understanding.

Often the universal patterns that govern the cosmos give messages through the soul. The soul warns you of such archetypal approaches and teaches what they demand. Warnings usually come through dreams or visions. The soul will try to keep you from harm or from directly facing what can be a formidable presence or force. When the archetypes (which are patterns or prototypes that reflect the laws that govern the universe) arrive and demand new growth, the soul is there to help. When the archetype shows up to impose karmic debt, the soul will try its best to convince you to participate freely and graciously, which of course is the wiser choice. It will help you do things you never thought you could do. This is because soul is in touch with levels of truth and wisdom, even power. Indeed, the soul itself is an archetype.

Try as we may, archetypes are not made by humans. Archetypes were here before us, and merely change shape over time to accommodate communication. They operate from a much higher and different sphere of understanding than we are used to here. Yet it is possible to understand them if we work with them. They are the carriers of the patterns and laws of the universe. All religions are composed from collecting archetypal information and relating these to the world. The soul is often the messenger through which archetypes speak. But archetypes are fully capable of communicating without the soul. Yet, since archetypes work harmonically with other archetypes and with all that exists, they work through the soul and other means, such as nature, to communicate their message. Angels are archetypes, gods are archetypes, the human form is an archetype, and DNA patterns are archetypes, etc.

We are living in exciting times when science and space studies, quantum physics, and metaphysics are combining to bring about new discoveries, new inventions, and new equations for experience and understanding.

We Experience the Soul Through the Virtues

The soul is both individual and collective. As noted above, it expresses itself through many means such as archetypes, symbols, and nature to name a few. But, most importantly, it expresses itself through human beings.

The soul has nurtured humankind since the beginning of time. It always brings one toward or back to harmony. Even though times are changing, harmony and homeostasis are always the souls beckoning. Let me address the virtues of the soul. There are many virtues that the soul enhances which include forbearance, brotherhood, compassion, knowledge, balance, wisdom, faith, hope, and love (to name a few). When we practice these virtues the soul illuminates. Eventually, one becomes an illuminated being because of one's beliefs and virtuous actions. Through the experiences of change the soul helps us find meaning in our everyday lives. The soul is always about the expansion of consciousness. It wants us to participate in life but through consciousness and the ability to see the bigger picture. At the same time, it wants us to clarify life through lived experience and knowledge. The soul desires us to experience life without losing touch with our own center and identity. That is what the virtues do for us. They keep us whole.

If someone is operating through life consciously, he or she is in touch with the soul. The soul is that center within us that maintains a connection with all that is around us. It helps us relate with the world at large, our interior psyche, and spiritual realms. This is spiritual homeostasis. But what is spiritual is often felt and manifests in our psychological and physical make up. Throughout history shaman have worked hard to heal spiritual, psychological, physical imperfections, and sufferings through enduring rituals and practices. Shamans are all about homeostasis or balance in our world. Their work is often to help a person balance their wounded psyche and ailing physical body. Shaman are meant to be agents of the soul and, we too, are meant to be agents of the soul.

The Soul Connects Us to Everything

Some religious traditions believe that the soul has a blemish to be accounted for or from which we need to be redeemed. Redemption is being aware that I am authentically free from sin. Redemption is the ability to love one another and forgive one another. Redemption is growth in consciousness. I do not believe that the soul needs to be awakened or needs to be washed clean, but that I need to be awakened to it. The soul is the spiritual aspect of myself that I participate in to connect to the Divine to aspire to higher levels of consciousness. It reflects Divine consciousness, and that consciousness is in every molecule and atom.

But the soul doesn't just enable me to climb the ladder of consciousness; it helps me aspire to become my authentic self in both the temporal and spiritual worlds. These worlds are real to the eyes of the beholder, and the soul acts as a communicator between them. But the soul is also that which gives me access to great beings, angels, teachers, guides, masters and the Divine. It is therefore the vehicle through which I receive wisdom and guidance. Hence, the soul is our guide through tenacious and difficult times. Therefore, we do well to maintain a connection with the soul to be sustained and guided by practical and spiritual wisdom.

Spiritual wisdom can be very practical. When I was in college, I had a dream where I was checking the oil level of my car engine. It showed to be very low. The next morning, remembering my dream, I checked the oil level in my car, and it was very low. I once dreamed that a raccoon came to me and asked, "Please put a bowl of water in your back yard. The weather has been so dry, and we are parched." I did so the next day, and raccoons, skunks and opossum all showed up late that evening to have a drink. These simple reminders are so important, yet they come through a spiritual or metaphysical means. If dreams can communicate the needs of animals, they can surely help us fulfill the needs of our families and all of humanity. Dreams are the language of the soul.

The Spiritual and the Tangible

We are in the world but not of it. This almost sounds like a preposterous statement. Many humans have difficulty coming to a sense of the spiritual while being in the material world. Being in the world but not of it is precisely where most people struggle, this is so because people experience and feel to be more of this material world than they are aware of the spiritual. Some personalities find it difficult to be in touch with the inner spiritual realms. But the fact remains that we are here in a human body. Yet, if one studies world religions and even alternative forms of medicine, the human body is shown to be a vehicle for connection to the spiritual and Divinity. But many people live their lives as though the material world is all there is. That is the crux of conventionalism. I believe that materialism is one of the reasons why there is so much suffering in our world. We do well to recall on a daily basis that we are spiritual beings in a physical world. There must be harmony between these two aspects of ourselves. Without harmony there is imbalance. Imbalance which if unattended can lead to a feeling of lack or suffering.

Many people on planet Earth are unable to connect with the soul because of an inability or refusal to forgive. These individuals need loving care from their community of friends. We are their community of friends. Helping others helps our world.

All world religions note that dedication to creating a better world is a noble path. We are asked by all religions to live noble lives of service while here in this body. To be of service to others changes the world we live in, balancing what is happening around us. Buddhism suggests we become compassionate. Islam suggests we ought to flourish as members of the brotherhood. Indigenous traditions and ways emphasize harmony with nature and all beings. Christian traditions teach that we are to love one another. Judaism teaches that God is an active participant in your life. Taoism and other Eastern traditions reflect wisdom that respects and encourages balance and order. The Hindu tradition calls us to devotion and seeks to treat all beings as sacred. The point of all of these virtues is that they bring us beyond the mind into the higher realms of being. They show us that we are representatives of not just the material world but of both the physical and the spiritual worlds. As long as we practice the virtues we are outside the ego's domain. The ego is the mind that is basically self-seeking. It separates us from others and therefore competes. Higher consciousness knows that we are all interconnected. The virtues understand interconnection and service.

Here are a few questions you may want to ponder. Are you dedicated to brotherhood, sisterhood, compassion, harmony, devotion, balance, or love? What, if any, is your religion? If not, what is your service, if any at all?

Ironically, through living virtuous lives people become arhats, saints, and Buddhas. When a Buddha or a realized person goes into the Land of Pure Light, what he or she sees and what he or she experiences is beyond illusion. Enlightened people experience what comes from the Spirit, the Buddha Mind, or the Christ Mind. Only love, purity, and harmony exist in that place. The potential for enlightenment is everywhere. It is within you and within every molecule. What seems so mundane contains divinity. What seems so inexplicable holds treasures and insights of wisdom. When the soul reflects itself to us, what appears to be common experience is transformed. Only by slowing down and releasing ourselves from the burden of the mind can we hear bits and pieces of what the soul is reflecting about.

Father Paul's Wisdom

Father Paul was an elderly Franciscan priest and a scripture scholar. He came into my life in 1980 during my novitiate year, which is the first year of entry into the Franciscan Order. Father Paul was a man of much wisdom. As a young priest, he experienced World War II in his home country of Lithuania. During that time, he was put under house arrest and confined to an eight by ten room. All they gave him was a Bible. During this time, Father Paul, a scripture scholar, commenced to memorize about one third to one half of the Bible. He became an incredible resource of information regarding the sacred scriptures.

Because Father Paul had an accumulation of study and life experience, I one day asked him if he had a message regarding the sacred scriptures that he would like to impart to me. He gazed at me and said, "Yes, I have a message about the sacred scriptures. But one must ask, which scriptures one is talking about – The Torah, The Bible, The Gita, The Mahabharata, The Vedas, The Koran, The Egyptian Book of the Dead, The Tibetan Book of the Dead, The book of Mormon. They are all scripture; I have read every one of them, and God speaks through all of them. Yet even more than that, God speaks through everything that exists. He speaks through every human being and animal that lives. He speaks through the plants, rocks and soil of the earth, and even the entire universe. It is all sacred, and it is all scripture. Every moment of every day God is speaking. Everything is the voice and word of God. The point of it all, more than anything else is, are you listening?"

Father Paul's words touched me to the depths. From his words my myopic world expanded to a vision that the Divine never ceases to communicate and does so continuously through every created thing. The visions I had from my youth immediately came to mind. Reflecting on them has often comforted me and brought me to that broader sense of Divine Presence and activity. Only by becoming still do these reflections speak to us. If you can still the mind, the soul reflects through you. When we meditate, the soul is reflecting and our connection to and participation with the Pure Light of the Creator Source is active. That is one of the main reasons for meditation. The Alchemy of soul is the ability to extract this Pure Light from one's experience of life. According to Webster, "Alchemy is a power or process of transforming something common into something special. It is an inexplicable or mysterious transmuting" (Miriam Webster). Alchemy can be a complex subject but also can be as simple as being inspired just by encountering a colorful bird, a strong tree, a gentle butterfly, or a familiar friend. The experience leads to transformation.

But this transmuting power has great healing potential. Do you remember a time when you felt out of balance and something brought you back to a place of harmony and peace? What brought you back? That was probably an experience of soul. The soul always returns us to our authentic selves. It gives us a sense of meaning in our world.

What works for me when I'm out of balance, or I've over-given, is a walk on the beach or in a forest, gazing at the beauty of flowers or of meadows, being with a dog or cat, or listening to music. But if I'm really hurting, I seek out my soul friends for companionship. There is nothing like a wholesome experience of community to restore us to our center. We are then able to refocus and discern again what really matters. Then we remember who we are again, we recapture our identity.

True Remembering

I know people who try to remember their past karmic lifetimes. Out of curiosity they are trying to recall who they were in other lifetimes. In 2002, I attended a talk given by Amrita, or Amma the hugging guru. A person in the audience asked her how to make up for all the bad karma of the past. Amrita responded saying that all one has to do is live by love in whatever you do and there is no longer a need to worry about karma. "Love," she said, "undoes the lifetimes of bad karma." I am reminded here of the Christian scripture, "Above all keep fervent in your love for one another, because love covers a multitude of sins." (1 Peter 4:8, New American Standard Bible)

Love activates the soul and leads directly to the Source of Pure Light from which we have come. In every, and any lifetime we have been influenced by love and by the soul, and through those two vehicles we remember who we really are. We are larger than most of us can handle. Why look at yourself from the point of view of lifetimes of the past? Instead, go to the source of who you are and always were. You are Light, and within that Light are governing laws, the highest of which is love. Light has within it an infinite desire to return to Itself. The desire to return to the Light is the action of the soul.

In a conversation I had with a Buddhist monk, he stated, "There is an array of power that wants to come to you. But it cannot come forth until you recognize it and achieve its beauty. It is with you always waiting to be discovered."

"Is it the Light of Lights?" I asked.

"Yes and no," he said. "No, because you have not yet fully realized it. Yes, because it is always waiting to be realized and known. The gift of everyone's life journey is to return to the Light."

What does the phrase, "return to the Light" mean to you? How might it be expressed in your life?

The Soul Reveals Itself

The soul expresses itself through many means. As noted above, archetypes, symbols, and nature likewise speak through the soul. This is the nature of a hologram. There is a Divine intelligence behind it, actually, running through it. But, most importantly from our point of view the soul expresses itself through human beings. The soul has nurtured humankind since the beginning of our creation. As a vehicle of spiritual homeostasis, it always brings us back toward our authentic identity. We are forever being restructured toward a higher awareness. Even though times are changing, harmony is always the souls beckoning.

The soul greatly desires that we live in harmony with all other beings while on this planet. It wants our peace and happiness. This is accomplished through a commitment to return to the glorious and virtuous Light. We do this through homage and by living virtuously in the world. When we practice the virtues the soul illuminates. Eventually, one becomes an illuminated being because of one's acclamation towards the Divine, and virtuous actions. This is what it means to experience expansion of consciousness.

The soul is always about the expansion of consciousness. It wants us to participate in life with the ability to see the bigger picture. It wants us to experience life without losing touch with our own center and identity, needless to say, our humanity.

One of my greatest concerns for today's society is that many people are losing touch with basic emotional and spiritual human needs. There are an alarming number of people who feel disheartened with society and where it seems to be heading. I often encounter people who have made choices that favor materialistic living, competition, or basic bad manners. Many people have no one to confide in and therefore feel separate. They need to keep looking for sustaining relationships. We all need to ask ourselves what sustaining relationships look like. We all need the support of wholesome friends.

A large number of my friends have complained to me that the daily news is no longer news. And Facebook is unsatisfactory in its lack of direction, in its lack of depth. Quite frankly, we are the ones who have to give all forms of media depth and a direction. The soul is never about separation or isolation, or an endless mantra of disillusioning news. If one is operating through life consciously, he or she is in touch with the positive aspects of the collective soul. The soul is that center within us that maintains a connection with all that is. It is that which balances and helps us to relate with the world at large and the worlds deep within. Many people are rather identifying with the collective trends in society, the result being unhappiness and fear. We need to redirect our energies toward a positive future. What manifests the future is how we are in the present. Further, we cannot manifest a positive future without the use of a creative imagination.

The Soul is the Imagination Reflecting

The soul is the imagination reflecting. It is also that which allows us and encourages us to relate with the Divine. The Divine permeates everything, because all that exists is a reflection of the Divine Source. Therefore, nothing is separate from it. We consciously connect to the soul through the imagination. If I align myself to the soul the soul becomes the imagination reflecting while in my body. It is an innate quality within us. In much the same way that the Divine imagines existence into being so do we. Since the Divine Source creates us, we share these qualities to imagine, reflect, relate, and create. Soul has much to do with the feeling aspect and all other subtle aspects of the human experience. These communicate to us our connection with the Divine and our experience of connection to ourselves and all other things and beings in the world. Ironically, much of this communication is done through still presence or meditation when the mind is quiet. That is when the soul communicates to us and through us best. There is much wisdom to be gained through present stillness.

Here is a reflection that came to me loud and clear after sitting in stillness for a time. The Gary mentioned in this reflection was a higher person than I. Somehow, I tuned into a higher part of myself, which had a message for me. During this meditation with stillness my mind became clear without a thought. Suddenly these words came forth: *A space has opened up in my heart. I am Gary and I am waiting for you to climb the ladder to meet me. We will open together a new space for creativity, and it will flow graciously out into the world. There is nothing that can stop you now. You have gone too far in the journey. All will be well! And, thank you for this time together.*

The importance of having a pen and notebook handy when going into prayer and meditation is evident. The above simple reflection came unexpectantly. But the time in which it came forth was profound for me. Allowing the imagination to self-reflect is important. That is how we hear or feel what it wants.

Bringing it Down to Earth

The soul is not a pie in the sky idea. Writing about our experiences helps ground them. They also help us look at them again and see what wisdom came through and when. Oftentimes, what I've written in my journal becomes food for thought or my sense of direction.

To bring our spiritual quest and experiences down to earth, we need to ask why do we have a soul? As stated above, the soul is a connection to ourselves, to all that is around us, and to the unseen forces that manifest in and around us. The Soul, as the connector of all things, helps us balance and make sense of our world and of our lives. It shows us how to relate to the Divine. It is the desire that leads us to the Divine. That's a lot.

To expand on the above ideas some of the aspects of soul are listed below:

A. The soul is an experience of the inner self. Yet, it encompasses all things and beings.
   1) Soul is found in the nature of being human
   2) Soul is a reflective experience
   3) Without a soul, we do not experience, intuit, relate, etc.
   4) Soul is a guiding component factor
   5) Soul is a guiding principle
   6) Soul is the Higher Self

B. There are numerous definitions of the soul both presently and from the past.
   - The soul as the polestar
   - The note of inspiration
   - The voice within
   - The urge to a life, a passion, or a calling
   - The connector to all that is
   - The connector to and of the Great Oneness of All Being
   - The conductor of energies

Some of the energies associated with soul include:
1. The feeling a parent has for a child or when holding an infant
2. The feeling a person has for a pet
3. The feelings that nurture partners, couples and friends
4. The feeling of walking on an ocean beach
5. The enjoyment of good food

6. The sense that good art or a good play instills in you
7. The sense that Fall, Winter, Spring, or Summer is coming
8. The feeling of connection to a tree, green grass, flowers, or a forest
9. The feeling when you stand before a vast open space or a mountain overlook
10. The feeling or sense that accompanies the sound of a running stream
11. That special place that somehow supports you
12. A special song that seems to always bring you home to yourself
13. The feeling or attraction to a favorite color
14. Some people have that sense with a thunderstorm or the sound of rain
15. Artists and writers are inspired with their creations and sometimes work tirelessly on their project
16. The experience of the virtues of compassion, brotherhood, harmony, and love
17. Music
18. Even the quest for the spiritual is seated in the soul
19. The list continues…

How Do You Experience The Soul?

Notice how all of the above experiences come through human life. Do the senses of the above experiences come to you through a knowing, a feeling, an intuition, a taste in the air, or through something you see or hear? Where in your body do you feel these? Through which chakra do you ponder the above questions (1 through 19)? Chakras are the energy centers of the body.

The Experience of Awe

Awe, or respect for what is ominous, is one of the doorways to a relationship with the Divine. The experience of awe often leads to a change within. More often than not, experiences of awe lead to homage of the Divine. Homage establishes a connection with the Divine, a deeper relationship. We also experience awe or a connection to the soul through profound premonitions, dreams, and visions. Some have experienced awe witnessing the peaceful death of a loved one or the birth of a baby.

There are other ways that the soul is experienced, such as through the awe of nature:
1. A clap of thunder
2. Pouring rain
3. Waking up to find the ground unexpectedly covered with new snow
4. An oasis in the desert
5. A high mountain
6. An avalanche
7. A thick forest
8. A flower or a field of flowers blooming

The Experience of Awe comes to us through many avenues. Encounters in nature are one of the ways we experience awe. Surviving a car accident unscathed can also bring us to a sense of awe. Through awe, we incorporate a sense of mystery, wonder, and attention. The feeling runs deep. It usually comes through an emotionally charged feeling of love, fear, a great pondering, or all of these at once. Sometimes an experience or new insight can be so powerful that it brings with it a sense of being struck. We never get over it and our life changes.

The experience of awe causes us to reflect suddenly and deeply and as the experience lingers, we give attention to what seems to have brought in the experience of awe. To give attention to something or someone is often a way of demonstrating love to the object of attention. When you want to show a friend or a child that you love him or her you spend time with your friend or child. This means that you are giving that child or person attentive presence. We relate to others, ourselves, and the world through attentive presence. People who do not relate well are often not attentive, either to themselves to others, or to the larger scope of life that is playing out before them.

What would it be like to give your soul attention or attentive presence? That's what meditation or a spiritual practice is all about. The experience of awe leads to reflection. As one ponders the experience, one also ponders the questions that enhance growth. According to Joseph Campbell, without awe we cannot know the soul or the Divine.

Mythology and Soul

Through the soul, we open ourselves to the world of mythology, story, fairy tales, fables, and lore. The ultimate goal of mythology is to move beyond myth and lore to a greater learning, a greater understanding, lesson, or teaching. Not only does the soul open us to the world of mythology and story, but mythology and story open us to the soul and its purpose in our lives and in the world.

The teachings of the Masters, the Buddha, the Hindu gods, and the Christ point to the great Oneness of All Being and how to be in the world. Simply put the great

Master teachers encourage us to live by brotherhood, compassion, harmony, service, and love. These virtues stimulate soul and soul responses.

Relating with the Soul

When the Divine is included as part of human development the soul is activated. If or when we reach out to soul it responds. The more energy we put into relating with it, the relationship deepens. It is an invisible but active force that runs through all things. It knows us intimately. It also knows all other things intimately. Through soul we open ourselves to the web that interconnects all things. Both the soul and we appear to learn through our activities. But our experience of the soul is that it has a task. It doesn't just sit around and do nothing. It is active and curious. Its purpose is to bring us to greater consciousness. Synchronistic events relay to us that soul is participating with us in our journey and guiding us through life.

What is Synchronicity

Synchronicity is a term coined by C. G. Jung. It points to instances when an event happens un-expectedly in union with a person's thoughts, desires, or needs in the moment. When a synchronistic event happens we must ask, what is the message? Synchronicity shows us that the universe is active in our lives and we are energetically and intimately connected to it.

Soul speaks through synchronicity utilizing dreams, visions, nature, animals, people, books, and objects through which it speaks. Synchronistic events show up at the right time. Perhaps a sound is made in the moment when something meaningful happens. Or a person or animal that represents the topic of discussion shows up. This means that Nature, other human beings, books as information and learning, all are significant to understanding the soul's messages and relating with the soul. We are part of a universe and the soul is inter-connected with it.

Something that happens to me very often is that I will hear a song from my past. When I stop to listen to the words of the song, I am awakened to a theme running through my life at the time. This can also happen with poetry or scripture. Often, I remember how a song, poem or scripture starts, but there is a message that relates to me when I hear the rest of the song or poem or Psalm.

Synchronicity communicates by many other means as well. When I was in graduate school at Catholic Theological Union, albeit with the chaos of that place, I managed to have a solid prayer life. One morning I awoke with thoughts of my friend Linda. Thinking nothing of it I performed my normal daily routine of prayer and breakfast, but thoughts of Linda came to me again. Even though it was early morning I felt to call her and see how she was doing. Linda and I talked for a few minutes over the phone and then I told her why I called and asked if she knew of a reason why she was on my mind. Linda said, "Gary I have here in my hand a bottle of pills that I was just about to take to end it all. That's why you felt to call me." It turns out that Linda told God that morning that if someone called her before 10 o'clock in the morning, she would not take the pills. She told me that she wasn't going to take the pills once I had called and wasn't going to tell me about the pills, but I had asked why I felt to call her. After some discussion, Linda allowed me to call a counselor friend of hers who lived not far away. Linda got the help she needed.

Linda received help because I had a connection to the Divine. But the same Divine Light in Linda was calling out to the universe for help. Through the soul connection, I was able to respond. I had no idea that Linda would have ever thought of doing harm to herself. Linda is presently a happy old gal in her upper eighties. The phone call I made to Linda was a moment of both Divine intervention and synchronicity. The hunch to call Linda was not a hunch at all but something far greater.

Do you recall moments when synchronistic events happened in your life? Was there a message that you received from the event?

An Early Morning Meditation

As a hospice chaplain, I find that my patients and their families sometimes show up in my dreams. Here is a story about a couple of my patients. It was about 4:00 a.m. and something – someone, a presence – jolted me awake. Something like a presence was pushed into my body. I was trying to understand what was happening, and then, in the dark of the night I saw a small female little person, about a foot high, standing in front of me. She abruptly stated, "Time to pray!" I didn't care for this message, as it was a day off for me, and in my mind that meant sleep in. The land of the soul doesn't always have days off when we want them. The Soul works when work is needed, and the Soul rests when rest is needed. Still in my stupor I could feel that the surplus junk that was slammed into my body did not feel pleasant. Naturally, I told it to get out. Another voice then said, "I ran out of energy." I then surmised that the surplus junk that was abruptly placed into my body (by a little person) was a human being. The realization came to me that someone ran out of energy and either wanted help or wanted my energy. I lay in bed for a time hoping the disturbing feelings in my gut and other parts of my body would go away but they did not. I then got up to pray, grumbling as I did so.

I began the meditation by just being aware of what felt like muck in my body. I then called upon my Angel and Christ and began to send white light through my chakras, my regular morning routine. After about two minutes I saw a person. It was Arlene. Arlene was a cancer patient who was terrified of death and didn't like to talk about death. She had been ill for some years and appeared to have the sympathy of her and her husband's families. For some unknown reason they all talked about her as though she were the most lovely and wonderful person. But when she was not in their midst, they were clearly very relieved. I experienced a different person from what they conveyed. The family members doted over her, and having been to her home, I saw the patient hurrying them here and there for her little needs. And, as soon as she received what she wanted, she would change her mind; she didn't need it after all. The little queen had them continuously scurrying for her.

I was invited to come to the patient's home to perform a meditation to help her calm down. The patient had been suffering from anxiety for weeks. She knew she was dying but refused to talk about her disease progression. She was literally trying to put death off which is not a wise thing to do, because, quite frankly, it is rarely possible. In her refusal to look at death she suffered from an unquenchable anxiety. In order to not deal with her anxiety, she commenced to being a very controlling person, ordering her family members here and there. Keeping herself and others busy had become her modus operandi so as not to discuss or look at death.

After observing all of these goings on in the patient's home I decided to try to learn more, if I could, and I wanted to be of help her and the family. I performed a meditation with the patient that she went into gleefully and beautifully. Arlene really liked the meditation experience and said that it lessened her anxiety. Then she said, "In fact, it was so good, you will come here every day to help me meditate." To which I immediately responded, "I will see you once every two weeks." One needed to have clear boundaries with this one!

After a time, I realized that Arlene was a sensitive soul who refused to look at or work with her own soul. Though very capable of soul searching, she wanted me to do the soul work she was responsible for doing. Arlene was afraid and lazy. She was able to entertain spiritual discussions about many topics and about others, but not about herself. She did not pray, or meditate, or ask soul searching questions of herself. Arlene had become materialistic as a means of convenience and escape. Yet, when I met her, she was facing the end of her life. I questioned that she might even be dying because she adamantly refused to do her soul work while on this planet. The energy of the soul is what keeps us alive and healthy, hence, our need to communicate with it and work with it.

While in my meditation, I learned that it was Arlene who awoke me at 4:30 a.m. It was her soul stating to me that it had run out of energy. People in her household and extended family have been doting over her because of her health issues for years. They were visibly tired and unable to play Arlene's game anymore.

I finished sending light through my chakras and called on my Angel and asked it to direct the meditation as it needed for Arlene. The meditation went on for a long time, as she did not want to leave the security of my body. I had to nudge her into the right place and encourage her to take steps in the right direction. She needed a lot of love.

As a chaplain, I personally refuse to be a ground for someone else's transition through death. I've done it too often before, and it is not a pleasant experience. I am happy to be a connection to Spirit and then release them after showing them where to go. I pray and ask protection that they find their way. But they have to make the actual trip themselves. It is surprising how many people who are dying ask me if there is a way that someone can go with them, so they do not have to make the journey alone. This is especially true of the uninitiated, that is those who failed to take risks or to be spiritually adventurous in life. It is sometimes true of marriage partners who have been happily joined for many years. They do not want to leave their loved ones. It is unthinkable, or perhaps frightening for them to entertain the idea to let go of the identity that twoness has given them.

The meditation had up to this point been focused on Arlene. As soon as she disappeared, someone else showed up, a good friend of mine who always over worked and taxed herself by giving too much. Again, I called upon my Angel and asked that it direct whatever needed to happen, this time for my friend Ellen. She had been warned to slow down. She had been encouraged to take time off for relaxation, prayer, and play. I hadn't spoken to Ellen in many months, but knew she was in trouble. A healthy person does not over-give or over-tax herself to the point of exhaustion. Ellen was not listening to her soul. She admitted to me that whenever the soul reached out to her, she could feel it, but her mind always told her that she had something to do. I grieved for her, sent her love, said prayers and released her to Spirit.

And so it is with the mystic. I had to deal with these people, and it was work. But that, at times, is my work. Arlene and Ellen were stuck because of their misguided beliefs and habits. They needed help. I believe that these two gifted people were meant to be part of the network that holds our planet in its proper order via contact with the soul. But neither are doing their work appropriately. One is refusing to work at all and the other is over working. A messenger from the spiritual web brought them to me in the wee morning hours. I trust the intense meditation was helpful for them, but how it affected them I do not know. I leave that in the hands of Spirit and released them.

After the eventful meditation, I was gentle with myself and nurtured myself to recover from the unusual, yet not so unusual, events of the early morning prayer.

Living Soulfully

Synchronicity is only one of the ways that the soul speaks to us. When we experience synchronistic events as messages from the Divine, we may also experience that we are intimately part of this universe and that the soul is relating to us. These are soul moments. Soul moments are moments in which we encounter the soul. To live soulfully means that we choose to have a relationship with the soul by how we live. One lives soulfully by keeping love or mindfulness in mind. Sometimes we do well to remind ourselves what love is and what it is not. This is also true of what it means to be mindful. Google dictionary states that mindfulness is "the quality or state of being aware or conscious of something. Used as a therapeutic technique, [it is] a mental state achieved by focusing one's awareness on the present moment, while calmly acknowledging and accepting one's feelings, and bodily sensations."

There is the saying that something or someone is en-souled. It is as though a spark of life is within it. To have lost soul refers to having lost that spark of life, that joy, that centering force which connects one to all other beings. We are en-souled when we are enmeshed with the notion and joy of the interconnection of all beings. I have found that human beings who are caught for long periods of time in deep sorrows or caught in addictions risk losing this interconnecting spark of life that centers and grounds them to the world. If taken literally, this means it is through a spiritual connection to the world about us that we are grounded. It is an innate voice of the heart that knows the interconnection between us and all other things spiritual and tangible. One recognizes it through expressions of joy, deeds of love, and compassion.

Having worked for many years in areas of poverty I was exposed to people who had difficult lives. I encountered prisoners, the homeless, and parishioners who were struggling deeply and appeared to have lost their center. A part of them had been damaged, as if the very part of them that held on to the joys of life or a belief that there is good in the world was lost to them. Sometimes my ministry required that I be for them what they could not be for themselves. This is challenging ministry.

One day a woman came to the parish who was fighting to keep her children. Her life had been exceptionally difficult. I did not feel that this woman was a bad person in any way. But she had made bad decisions during her life, the accumulations of which haunted her. She would come to me for counseling sessions but it was as though she was unable to remain centered to process her life and the situations she was encountering. If I asked her questions, she would immediately go off into a list of fears of what might happen to her if things didn't happen in her favor. She had lost that point within that holds us all together. She was not able to ground herself in reality. She had lost that centering power of love and joy. She had lost her connection to herself that gives a peaceful perspective. The only way I could help was to remain present. If I held presence, it usually took about 20 minutes before she would calm down and think somewhat sensibly again. But this wounded soul needed someone to be with her and be present for much of her day. Sadly, she was no longer capable of being a mother because she was not able to make wholesome decisions for herself, hence, clearly not for others.

The Soul is a powerful grounding force through which the Divine Light is brought into the micro-cosmos. Presence allows for this grounding force to happen. If we are able to be present with others and ourselves we have not lost our connection to the soul. That flame is what gives us a sense of the center-point out of which we operate. The divine flame is with us and will ignite those around us as well.

Living a Soulful Life in the World

If a person wants to live soulfully, there are questions to consider. Who do you hang out with? Where do you hang out? What brings you to those places? What do you call fun activities? Do you take time out to just be present to yourself and others?

Notice that some people do not think the way you think or share the same ideas of what is fun. What makes you unique? What bonds you to your friends? What do you do together that creates friendship? Every individual relationship that you have is a reflection of aspects about yourself.

After looking at the above questions, we realize that who we spend time with, where we spend time, and what activities we choose to participate in come from choices that we have made. The ability to make choices is an act of power. Your choices ultimately define who you are in the world. Until you make different choices you cannot change who you are. Hence, choices directly create your self-image as well as directly influence your relationships with others and the Divine.

Walking Soulfully

As stated in the Introduction:

> To walk soulfully you need to desire to know who you are. Who are you authentically? To walk soulfully you need to desire to be on the path toward your authentic self. It may take more than half a lifetime to learn who you are authentically.
>
> Have you ever considered what your life-path or calling looks like as seen from the eyes of the Creator?
>
> How do you learn what your life-path is? It's one thing to know your life-path, but to what depth do you know it? Do you know it just mentally? Do you know it with understand-

ing? Are you willing to know it, or already know it in your emotional being as well as intellectually? Some people emotionally feel their calling but do not understand it intellectually.

To know the above, that is your whole life's journey right there!

To walk soulfully is to experience your inner-self and its desired response to the world. This means being conscious of the world you are in without being wrapped up in fleeting desires and dramas.

What are Soul Moments?

Soul moments are moments in which we encounter or experience the soul. We are present in the moment and glean from it what it has to bring us. A soul moment may be a moment just for that moment. Or, it can be a moment that if held and reflected on can nurture and nourish us through life. We all need nourishing moments. Such possible moments include:
- Holding a baby
- Becoming a parent or grandparent
- An experience in meditation
- The feeling of peace while in nature
- Your child graduates from high school or college, or gets married
- You have a deep feeling of trust when speaking with someone
- A sense of awe from any source (a conversation, an insight, a tender loving animal, a feeling of beauty or love or gratitude, the fruits of the spirit) these are all

ultimately from Source
- A delicious savory meal
- An inspired sermon
- Community, and relationships
- You experience a moment when knowledge and wisdom are infused into your mind and body
- You sense yourself going deeper, going wider, going higher
- The wonder of the invisible worlds
- You feel a calling to do something
- A friend calls or visits you when you are feeling lonely or down

The importance of soul moments is that many of them are experienced through making a choice. We cannot have an experience in meditation if we do not meditate. We cannot have an experience in nature unless we put ourselves there. We cannot receive knowledge and wisdom unless we look for it by reading, watching informative videos, or talk with the right people. We cannot experience an inspired sermon unless we are attached to a church with a good pastor. Having quality family time is also a choice. We need to create time for these things. If a person chooses to do just some of the above five examples, he or she will probably have a much fuller life and will experience soul moments that sustain them through life. The more we nurture ourselves with soulful moments the more that soulful moments happen naturally in our lives. We become deeply touched by events around or within ourselves.

Can you tell me about a soul moment that you've had in the past that still nurtures you today when it comes to mind?

What empowers you?

Making Choices

If you wonder what it means to live a soulful life, then you may wish to ponder some of the daily choices you make. What do you wake up to in the morning?

a) Texting? The radio? TV programs? The News? Computer? Facebook? Twitter? A newspaper? Or do you wake up to...

b) Meditation? Yoga? A walk with nature? Sacred reading? Journaling? Looking at your dreams? Spiritual presence? Coffee or tea and reflection? Walking the dog? Being with your spouse and children? Children can also attune one to the higher vibrations. The daily practices mentioned in groups "a" and "b" are choices we make. Positive choices can help you experience what it means to be in touch with the soul and these routine practices can help you grow higher on the spiritual path. They are healthy habits. You may have noticed that all of the life habits in group "b" require intention and attention if one is to grow spiritually or grow in consciousness.

c) Many people wake up to a spouse and children and all that that involves. This can be a spiritual experience for some but many experience it as a chore, or a duty of love. Some consider it a burden. Working with family members always demands intention and attention. There are some people who love being mommy or love being daddy. Keep in mind that parenting is about being a parent. It's not just about a feeling of accomplishment because it feels good being mommy or being daddy; or, because it may look good to others.

Having children is an archetypal pattern that fulfills a sense of duty to society. This means there is a powerful feeling within us to become parents and procreate. But this act needs to be done consciously. If not, your children may become outward projections of your unfulfilled lives. How we perform as parents is a choice. Kahlil Gibran, in his book, <u>The Prophet</u>, states that children are a gift from God, they are not your property. You must chose to not place onto your children your own unfulfilled thoughts and desires. Rather, treat your children as though they belong to God. Gibran provides deep thought for us to ponder:

> And a woman, who held a babe against her bosom said,
> Speak to us of Children.
> And he said:
> Your children are not your children.
> They are the sons and daughters of Life's longing for itself.
> They come through you but not from you.
> And though they are with you yet they belong not to you.
> You may give them your love but not your thoughts.
> For they have their own thoughts.
> You may house their bodies but not their souls,
> For their souls belong to tomorrow, which you cannot visit,
> not even in your dreams.
> You may strive to be like them, but seek not to make them like you.
> For life goes not backward nor tarries with yesterday
> (Gibran, Kahlil. *The Prophet.* New York: Alfred A Knopf, Inc. 1979. p. 18-19).

But the poet continues by addressing the path and blessings that parents experience:

> You are the bows from which your children as living
> arrows are sent forth.
> The archer sees the mark upon the path of the infinite,
> and he bends you with his might that His arrows may go
> swift and far.
> Let your bending in the Archer's hand be for gladness;
> For even as He loves the arrow that flies, so He loves also
> the bow that is stable (pp. 18-19).

Since children belong to God, the wiser person will pray to God for their protection, guidance, and strength each day? Parents also well to pray and give thanks that they are able to provide for their children and family. Such a prayer is an intention.

What is an Intention?

An intention is having a purpose in mind to bring about a healing, a wholesome habit, a change in our lives, or to manifest something. Intention places attention into something for our own or another's benefit. Hence, we always do well to make an intention just before we perform a daily practice. Many spiritual leaders suggest the importance of making an intention for the day as soon as we wake up in the morning.

The quality of giving attention to someone or something, or even to an aspect of oneself means to consider or contemplate, study or observe, leading to awareness. If one is aware of something or someone then appropriate action easily follows. The psyche naturally feeds into what we give attention or aspire to. Attention also is associated with being present. One becomes aware and present through a spiritual practice.

What Does it Mean to Have a Practice?

A spiritual practice is a daily discipline that one participates in for the purpose of spiritual growth and possibly the completion of a goal, such as happiness, physical health, financial gain, a diploma, emotional calm, body balance, a relationship with God, etc. For Sadhu's and guru's, their relationship to the Divine is their practice, because that is the strength that nurtures everything else in their lives. For those who are more mundane in their approach to spiritual living, the spiritual practice is a choice made to better their lives. Without a practice, we will not be able to sustain our spiritual and physical energies in the face of what is happening on this planet both now and in the near future. From a spiritual perspective, a relationship with the Divine is crucial for well-being and happiness. We must raise our vibrational levels to higher frequencies to attain the guidance and strength we need. This demands a commitment to a spiritual practice.

A daily spiritual practice is key to working with the soul. Having a practice is how we get to know the soul and how it works for us and within us. A practice is an ongoing continuous training to increase or improve spiritual awareness and states of being. It helps us to be ready to experience Divinity in many forms. Performing a spiritual practice is therefore a discipline that generally requires a goal, an aspiration to become or be in touch with higher spiritual awareness. When an aspiration is identified and daily spiritual practices are performed, parts of the participant will begin to awaken.

Those parts of us that are awakening sometimes access intelligence beyond our thinking capacity. A spiritual practice puts into activity a seat of wisdom that is beyond our daily clamoring mind. This seat of wisdom is within us, and it is beyond the thinking brain. If there is a meeting with the seat of wisdom on a regular basis, it will bring a sense of order to the spiritual journey.

Stilling the mind, is the road to a guided spiritual journey. If a practice of quieting the mind is in place, the wisdom beyond the human thinking brain speaks and directs the life of the incumbent. Meditation and yoga then become ways to access a way of being in the world. One is in the world but not of it as one is still here but less controlled by what is here. Rather, one is guided through the soul connection to the greater mind, the Divine Mind. This serves as both sanity and protection. It does not mean we will have less suffering, it means that we have the potential to be free from it. To hold the suffering of the present world, as it affects you individually, in present stillness is the gift. Why? When the mind stops, the inner wisdom, the inner watcher, will heal it, transform it, or give you a direction of action perceived through or beyond it. Through experience with the soul in stillness or meditation, new ways of thinking and being in this world will be shown or brought to you. One is nurtured with wisdom. Everything becomes a lesson.

Doing the Work: Being Ready

How do we know that we are ready to embrace a life with soul?

1. Having an open mind is important because then one can develop a mind that is receptive to Divinity and how it works. We like to limit the Divine. We like to say

to Spirit, "I'll have it, or do it, but my way." Very often messages come to us and we say, "No," "Not yet," "I'll do it tomorrow," "I don't have enough money," "I don't have enough time," "Impossible," "Over my dead body," "If you give me the end result first (of a house, a home, the vacation I've always wanted, fame, fortune, or the recognition I deserve), then I'll get on with doing what you want me to do." "Just let me have one more reckless fling." Those are the things we often tell the Divine when we are invited to live a soulful life.

2. Looking back to when I was a pastor of parishes; The greatest failures I have had when I was a pastor were when I did not listen to Divine instruction:

A. I did not say something that needed to be said because I did not want to hurt someone.

B. I did not do something in the parish because I was afraid to do it. It was all new to me and I was afraid of making mistakes.

C. I didn't believe in myself. That I could actually do it.

D. I didn't hear the message because I was too tired doing all the things that I thought others, or I myself, expected me to do. I was holding on to an image of status quo using of all my energy in the process. A parish without change is bound to become stagnant. Our world is rapidly changing. So too must the church and its parishes and parishioners. One has to be in a healthy dialogue with all of the new experiences that are influencing the current world. This is a huge task. It may be a formidable task when you consider that the psychological make-up of the average Church attender does not care for change.

E. I sought to receive affirmation because there was so much that was lacking or incomplete within myself.

F. I failed to take time to meditate properly as I could

have.

G. I was not present in the moment.

There are certain moments, certain opportunities, that come our way that are sacred, and we can totally miss them if we are not awake and aware. While in that moment, we must trust that all will be well. When these moments pass us by, they pass us by, possibly never to be seen or heard again. We can only look back and wish that we had responded to the call of the moment.

The good news is, if we do not give up, the soul never gives up on us, no matter what! It interconnects us with the Divine. The second that we ask forgiveness and reconnect ourselves to soul and the Divine, we are right back where we are supposed to be. If we are influenced by Divinity, most mistakes are lessons to be learned so that we can move on to greater lessons. Some mistakes are grave and have to be accounted for. Even then, the Divine is waiting for us to return and get on with the journey. There is much to do and little time within which to do it. This means that every moment is an opportunity to serve.

A note of comfort is to remember that you are made of the Divine Essence. You are entwined with the life of the universe. This means that you are never alone.

Choices, Identity and Persona

When choices lead to healthy habits, we are on the right path. What you do, the daily habits you practice, and your activities create the image you have of yourself and that others have of you. How do you present yourself out in the world? What is the persona that you wear out in the world? Personas are the images that you put on as you go through life. What is the persona that you wear when you are by yourself at home? What is the persona that you wear when at work? The average person expresses themselves through at least five different personas. Most of us present ourselves to the world through even ten or more personas. Have you ever thought about what your major or most important personas are?

The following questions will help you learn what your personas are. Knowing your personas is extremely important. Personas have to do with your personal image and the images and skills that you bring to the world.

What image do you want others to have of you? What image do you have of yourself? What is your profession? Do you like your profession? What words do you use when you speak? How do you dress? Are you a vain person and if so why? What is your reason for wearing the clothes you do? Do you wear clothes for others to see you or for you to feel like you are being yourself? What inspires you? What are your hobbies? What do you do for fun? What do you do for fun with others, and what do you like to do when you are alone?

These are consciousness-growing questions that help us be aware of and understand ourselves. There are many other questions we could ask about the reasons behind the choices we make. But, answering the above simple questions allows us to make choices and decisions that shape our spiritual and material lives. These great and small decisions also have to do with what gives us meaning. Hence, the questions that answer why we do what we do, when, with whom, and how, are private ponderings that lead us to the profound statement "know thyself." Ultimately all of your personas, meaning all of the images that you carry of yourself and project to others, affect your life with the soul.

Having pondered the images that you have of yourself, are you perhaps aware of those that you present to the world? Would the feeling be wonderful, interesting, or frightening to really know what others think or perceive about you? Unfortunately, many of us are only sometimes aware of the image that we portray to the world. Many of us believe that we are portraying a particular image to the world but what do others perceive? The less we know of or about ourselves, the less we know about the soul. This is because the soul works through the images we choose to portray. If the images are false or not true to our Divine calling, then they cannot be applied to a relationship with the soul. Also, more than likely, the less we know about ourselves the less contact we have with our own soul and the less we know our authentic self. The Persona is the public image a person presents to others. It is also the personality, the identities, or roles that are perceived by others. It is an exterior image that one portrays to the world but is not necessarily the internal you.

Hence, knowing yourself is so important. We all have a number of personas that we wear when at home, at work, while alone, or while out-and-about. A human being needs at least five well-developed personas in order to function as a healthy human being. A persona is the part of your personality that you project out in the world for others to experience or see. It is the character that is perceived by others of you when you are out in the world. In other words, you may not even be aware of a persona that you project to others, or that others project onto you. That's kind of scary isn't it?

Let me give you some examples of personas and how they help us, or entrap us:

1) There is **Gary the writer**. This is an important part of myself through which I relate to the world. While writing, I actually feel that the world is relating to me. Writing is a form of mental health for me. Through writing, I am able to clarify my deepest thoughts. I express myself through writing. A part of me is going out into the world. At the same time, in order to write I have to go within and reflect. Writing offers creative expression, which offers the sense of fulfillment and accomplishment.

2) I also am **Gary the teacher**. In all honesty, I am born to teach. Writing helps me with my teaching profession. Teaching is one way in which I relate to, or interact with people in the world. It gives me a sense of fulfillment. Teaching allows me to help others, which is a gratifying experience. It challenges me to want to know more, study more, reflect, and experience more. Being a teacher has become my greatest means for learning. Teaching demands that I continuously study new information. I enjoy helping others learn.

3) I am **Gary in a relationship**. Who I am at home with my partner is important to me. It takes work to be in a relationship, and I believe that both Will and I have a healthy balance of relating as partners. There are some things that we'd each individually like to see improve in our relationship. But sometimes improvements as I call them or as he calls them aren't happening. Yet, despite our differences, we are growing together, and we each take on particular roles wherein we are able to use our gifts to support the relationship. I believe that we both relate well in most aspects of our partnership.

When we go through our individual and shared hells, I feel that we do a particularly good job of supporting each other. Relationship helps us share beyond ourselves. And this type of sharing creates yet a deeper bond. Will and I have a lot of deep discussions about what is happening in our world, about our nighttime dreams, about our hopes and dreams as a couple about our work and relationships, etc. I have a fulfilling relationship. Wilhelm has been and continues to be, by far, my healthiest blessing and greatest challenge. My relationship brings about a lot of homeostasis for both of us. Because of our relationship, we are both better human beings and we are able to be active creators, teachers, and healers affecting the lives of others in the world. Wil is my soul-mate.

4) I am **Gary who is nurtured by nature**. I love to spend time walking in nature, being with nature and with others in nature. At the same time, I deeply need and love to be alone in nature. Through nature I commune with the world. When I need to be with all that is in the universe in its purity, I go to nature. This clarifies me to myself, restores me to who I am and what my purpose is in the world. I may have great burdens, but being in nature helps me to process them and let go of them. Nature does this quickly for me. Nature restores my soul.

5) I am **Gary the Spiritual Counselor**. I am currently a hospice chaplain. Much more could be said about this profession. At this time, I choose to not elaborate about my work as a spiritual counselor to patients and families because I am going through a lot of change within this profession. My identity as a hospice chaplain is changing.

6) I am **Gary who meditates.** I awaken every day before sunrise. If I do not awaken, I am often awakened by elementals and told, "It's time to pray." My day

begins with meditation and prayer and ends with prayer. That is how my life has been since age seventeen. At that age, my cousin, who was a friend, and classmate was shot to death in front of me in a gun accident. I received an awakening and a sense of urgency to commence to prayer and meditation. My life has not been the same since.

Nothing leads to gratification quicker than meditation, as it releases stress and re-centers a person in a life with the soul, our means of communication with the Divine. But meditation is a discipline that needs to be a regular daily event for it to be fruitful. A relationship with the Divine is what taps us into our authentic gifts and talents as well as the calling that we are given to manifest while on earth. The soul is our connection to all other beings. Meditation is one of the soul's paths.

7) I am Gary the **former Catholic priest.** This is a powerful archetype, which carried with it a lot of responsibility. Priesthood carries with it many projections that others put onto a priest. In some cultures, priests are loved. In other cultures, priests are not loved, depending on the history of that location. While I was an active Catholic priest, my job required that I work many hours a day. There was an expectation that I not use swear words. While I was a priest every word was measured. There was an expectation for me to be a loving person. In some areas where I did ministry children were not allowed to be close to me. In other areas, I was asked to be with the children, teach them and love them. When I lived in Mexico, some people grabbed my hands and kissed them.

I found that being a priest isolated me. I had to be conscious of what others were thinking about me and how I was being received at all times. It is a continuous pressure that one deals with. Yet, at the same time, one is commissioned with the tasks and duties that come with the role, the image of priesthood.

When I was a priest, there were parts of me that really and truly loved being of service to others. When I was on the altar, I always asked God that an inspired message would come through for the people. It was a matter of compassion. I had to literally forget all the projections that were being placed onto me, as well as those that I had placed onto myself. In doing so, I found that quite often something magical happened and people felt touched, renewed or ministered to. It was as though I became a blank slate, like a glass window, to allow the light of God to shine through. That is what I would ask for. (Was that an illusion of my ego?) In other words, priesthood for me was literally the ministry of being available, first to God as a human being and then to those I served. When able I enjoyed stepping out of the way for the Divine to come through. That is something I still do in my personal ministry, meditation and prayer.

But this writer suffered from the jealousy of other priests because of my successes. They projected onto me their failures. The people in the pew also placed burdens onto me that were not mine to carry but theirs to carry. Some of them saw me as some kind of magical being that because they felt happy or peaceful in my presence, it was expected that I be available more than I was able to be available. Yet, I often held the expectation of myself to be available at all times to others, which is one of the reasons why I burnt out.

One must also be aware that there is very little comparable to the wonderful education one receives during the period of training to become a priest. I was lucky to have had very good teachers and good superiors. Many priests are not so lucky. They are either limited or blessed by their education and their ability to process life and love.

Much more could be said about the persona and priesthood.

9) I am **Gary, a person who is gay.** The most difficult part of my life has been that of being a gay person. I was raised on a farm about six miles from a small town in Nebraska. I was not aware of any other people who were gay from that area of the world until I had been gone from it for about five years. Quite frankly, I just never knew what to do with myself or for myself. Being gay wasn't talked about in that small town. I certainly wasn't going to bring it up. I was filled with a sense of being separate from everyone else. A deep loneliness accompanied my youth and has carried into adulthood. In all honesty, I just always tried to fit in, whatever that meant at the time.

Then one fine day when I was a junior in high school, I made a comment to a classmate. I have no idea what it was that I said, but the Franciscan nun in charge of the class said loudly for all to hear, "Well that's because you're gay, Gary." I was dumbfounded and didn't know what to do or say in return. She repeated it three times, and everyone just looked at me. From then on, there were occasional remarks, not from the guys, but from the female members of my class. These remarks were always unexpected and hurtful. My defense, which was no defense at all, was to hear what was said, and then just ignore it and go deeply within. Each time something like that happened, isolation and confusion crept in.

My gayness wasn't dealt with until I went to the

Franciscan seminary at age twenty-two. There I could talk about being gay with my spiritual directors – some who were good and some who definitely were not. Sexual contact was strictly taboo in the seminary. It wasn't openly talked about, and I surely wasn't going to go there with my classmates. There was someone I loved among my classmates, but he wasn't open to being sexual with me. I made mistakes and lost our friendship. So deep unfulfilled sexual feelings lingered within and haunted me. My college seminary years just didn't allow for an experience of sexual freedom with another human being to happen. I was curious, fearful, and certainly needy, but never fulfilled. So I ignored it. Yet, once again, while my gayness was held a secret by me, for some reason ever body knew I was gay. What I held secret was a known persona for others to see. The personas I thought I projected was that of being a very good person and also being a spiritual person. I was blind to myself.

By my second year in theology, I came to realize that I could talk about my personal life with a few trusted friends. I was shocked to learn that at least 70 percent of the seminary students were gay. Coming out was a gradual and painful process for me. Being gay had so many implications and should-nots applied to it. One was guilty, always guilty, no matter what you did or didn't do. A gay person is marked by both the church and society. We are convenient targets because we represent what society doesn't want to look at. Gay people represent the people who live on the margins of society, the ones society doesn't want to deal with.

My first experience of sex happened when I was in theology when I was a master's student. Someone took an interest in me and moved the relationship into a sexual relationship. A lifetime of pent-up feelings came to the fore and I became aware of love and pleasure as well as that of being a mess of desire. Worse, after opening me up to sex, my sexual partner wanted to step out of it. I was left with all those unresolved feelings. I lived in a community of men and there were many other communities of religious men close by. Most all of the students were gay, but since we were members of the institutional church where celibacy is a must, all sexual activities were done in secret. I was ignorant about what was happening around me and yet needy. So I lived with a face of guilt, because I so wanted to learn about it and to experience sexual freedom. I meditated daily and sincerely and performed all of the duties and prayers expected of me. Yet I was probably an open book of need wherever I went. I do not know how I got through those years. I nurtured myself by many long lonely walks beside Lake Shore Drive.

But I wasn't the only one carrying the persona of the seminarian theologian. The seminarian takes on a persona where one is expected to put on an image of perfection to the world while being young, vibrant, and celibate. Can you imagine the testosterone that was ready to flare up at any given moment? The secrets, the gossip, the slander, guilt, and shame that were woven through those years are beyond belief. Somehow, I made it through and into priesthood. To this day, I still question what it means to be a sexually healthy person.

The positive side of being a gay person was that compassion for others came naturally for me. Because of my experiences as a gay man, I was able to feel and understand deeply into the lives of the stranger. Because I myself lived on the edge of society it was easy to empathize with those who lived on the margins of society. For that reason, I turned out to be quite a good minister.

But the journey of my reckoning with being gay and coming out about it was a long and painful road. Being gay is not a choice, and I wouldn't wish it onto anyone. I am grateful when I encounter young guys and gals in their teens who are gay and appear to be happy with their lifestyles. But many are not happy; they do not feel accepted in their families or by their peers. To this day, I really just don't talk about being a gay person with my family. Most of them have stated to me that my gayness doesn't matter to them. But I simply do not have personal relationships with my siblings and relatives to the degree that I'd feel free to dialogue about such a deep subject. My journey was too difficult and too alone for too long. It's not that the love was and is not there. Rather, my journey took a unique, singular, difficult path. If it were not for a naturally deep spirituality I might have perished.

Today, close friends with whom I can discuss most any topic nurture me. I am free and have been able to let go of many bruises. I am no longer haunted by my identity. Most importantly, I no longer look to others for approval, which was always a set-up for emotional failure. I no longer feel guilty about myself, or my life. I have carried hard-earned lessons that were eventually nurtured into wisdom. Namely, I have begun to move beyond trying to identify with personas, those of others as well as my own. I have learned that personas are steps in growth. I have learned that any unfulfilled life, be it a gay, celibate, or simply an alone person, often causes one to go beyond the physical for meaning and pleasure. It is not a fun or easy process by any means, but once you have arrived there, why would you return to seek physical pleasure except for love? Rather, I try to identify with my soul and its desires. The compassionate soul realizes that beyond personas is a living human being, a person, a heart that has needs, aspirations, and desires. If a person gets to the core of these through a path of love the seat of one's true identity shows its face. Beauty is then restored to the once imprisoned soul. Eventually, one learns that identity ultimately comes from living a virtuous life.

Other personas that I carry that will not be expounded on here are:

10) I am **Gary with a farmer background, it's in my bones**

11) I am **Gary who loves to experience other cultures**

12) I am **Gary who loves to study spirituality**

13) I am **Gary who sometimes enjoys cooking**

14) I am **Gary who sometimes enjoys shopping**

15) I am **Gary who sometimes enjoys cleaning house**

What are your personas, the images that you carry out into the world? It is healthy to know them.

We all have personas similar to those listed above. They are continuously with us. But what might it mean for you to question the nature of the personas that you have taken on? For instance, what might it mean to identify with your soul's desires instead of your persona's? We begin to do this when we ask the question: What does my soul want of me? If you are a parent, you already have the desire from Spirit to be a good parent. We are all responsible for what we bring into this world. Whatever your profession, the divine desires you do it well. When we ask the questions, what does my soul want of me we move from persona to icon.

The icon is infused with light, like the stained-glass window that shows its colors when the sun from the other side reflects through the window. An icon is a reflection of, a representation of, something greater than we are. When we ask what the Divine or the soul wants of us and take action in the world from that perspective, that Light shines through us. The whole idea of Orthodox Church icons is that since they are two-dimensional images, the icon can only become complete when someone prays with it. The person who gazes at the con becomes the third dimension. In three-dimensional reality, something is actualized. This means that something in the image, quality, or presence conveyed by the icon is made actual in the worshiper. One's life is changed.

Think about it. There are medical doctors, janitors, farmers, nurses, and computer scientists who are brilliant at what they do. They don't have to talk about God. As conscientious beings the light already shines through their work and through who they are as human beings. And then there are those who just do not seem very in touch with what they are doing. I know many people who are not happy in their professions. People who perform their work consciously tend to be considerate of others and tend to do their work well. People who are not happy with their work and have not reflected as to why, often do not treat themselves or their clients as well as they could. Hence, there are fewer fulfillments. Those who are unhappy in their professions would do well to ask to be guided by their soul to their authentic life purpose. But do not ask that of the Divine if you are not willing to change! We are living in a powerful time. We have completed our time beyond the Mayan calendar. This is a potent time as we have officially stepped into a new aeon, the Age of Aquarius. Furthermore, we have completed the 26,000-year cycle of the horoscope. Something totally new is emerging, and much of what we knew in the past is disintegrating. Energies are and have been potent since about 2008. This will continue up until about 2034 or longer if you have raised your levels of consciousness. If you are tuned into this profound moment in history, you can ride the energies toward higher consciousness and awareness. Stilling the mind every day or just being with your breath can become powerful exercises. Be careful what you ask for during this powerful time, but once you have clarity about what to ask for do ask. Be brave. Move forward on the spiritual road if you can.

Unhealthy Personas

Questions for reflections: If you are a Christian, what personas do your place onto Jesus, the Holy Spirit, and God? Is what you expect of them fair to them?

What personas and expectations do you place onto your rabbi, priest or minister? What personas do you place onto your family members, co-workers, your boss, etc.? Are you being fair to them? What personas do others place onto yourself?

For us to develop spiritually, we need to be aware of the personas that we carry and that we project onto ourselves and others. If we know our personas, we know our gifts, and we also know our shortcomings. When we familiarize ourselves with our personas, we can become aware of how others perceive us. Personas represent helpful tools that are imbedded in our individual personalities. But part of working with the personas we carry requires being aware of which ones are healthy and which ones are not.

I know a gentleman who looks like Santa Claus. Every year he thoroughly enjoys playing the role of Santa at the local stores and mall. However, during the past five years he has worn bright red colors throughout the year wherever he goes. My friend Max has taken on the Santa archetype as his own personal persona. He wears a bright red velvet cowboy hat. It's a handsome hat that matches his pure white long sleeve shirt with bright red suspenders, red pants, and black boots. But all year round? One has to question who the real Max is behind all that red. I always enjoy talking with him when I see him, and I know just how much he loves the Christmas season and his gift of playing the role of Santa during the holidays, but I haven't been able to get to the real person behind the Santa suit. I have no doubt that Max is a generous soul, as he helps people throughout the year as a volunteer in food shelter programs, with people who live on the street, etc. It appears to be a fact that Max has become a year-round Santa.

I also question when I encounter people who talk about their favorite ball team year-round. Not only do they talk about it, but they wear the supportive clothes representing that team wherever they go. Ball teams are seasonal, not year-round. This means that taking on the role as a team supporter appears to be a safe place for the year-round sports team supporter. But one must question, is there not more to life than football, basketball, baseball, or Santa Claus? It is healthy for us to question what images we have taken on and why. If you take on an image so strongly for all to see, is it possible that the deeper parts of the soul have not been nurtured? In other words, who is the real person that lies beneath the image we wear in public?

Having been educated through the seminary system,

I was often exposed to the question as to who I authentically was as an individual. That is one of the gifts that manifests from schools of liberal arts. I have learned that the gifts I have for others have come to me from having been without those very gifts at some point in my life. The absence of something that is needed often creates knowledge of and about it. I have met people who did not receive affirmation and acceptance during their childhood years, yet they are some of the most affirming and caring people to be around. They have learned how to be what others need. They know how to make whole in others that was so lacking in themselves. Some people carry these wounds for life, yet, no one is aware of it. The projected image (the persona) is that of being whole to make others whole.

We all have negative personas. Unhealthy personas are ultimately undeveloped self-images. Sometimes we put on the image or persona of someone who loves shopping but to be a shopping addict is a persona with an entrapment. These are two very different personas. Another example is that while I sometimes love to cook, shop, and clean, there are times when those are the last activities I want to perform. Can you imagine how I feel when I am pressured to have to do these things when I don't have time to do them? But house cleaning is a short-term thing that comes my way on a weekly basis. Can you imagine if you burn out of a particular life profession, yet have to return to work every day performing what you no longer like? When you have to take on an image that you do not like and have no option but to continue living that image, you will burn out. It has been well noted that most Catholic priests who left the priesthood, left not because they lost their vocation, but because they burnt out. Once a vocation, which is a persona, is burnt out, it will more than likely not be used again. The image is done. Like a piece of clothing that has been worn too much for too long, it has holes, has become frayed, is coming apart, and no longer fits your character, even if you were good at it. The persona must change. It has lost its vigor and strength to perform. It has lost its joy.

I definitely had some sort of burnout before I left the priesthood. I was mentally, emotionally, spiritually, physically, and even psychically exhausted. I spoke with a doctor about how I was feeling. She recommended me to a good spiritual director and then proceeded to tell her story. When acting as a physician in Alaska, she was flown by airplane from village to village. But the need was great, and she could not keep up unless her days exceeded eleven hours at six days a week. Eventually, she burnt out.

Being a deeply spiritual person, she went to a spiritual director who explained that when we are born, we are given only a certain amount of energy. The young physician learned that she must not over give or she would run out of energy. But the experienced spiritual director informed the medical doctor of a spiritual life-sustaining secret. If we have over given and our life force is gone, we will have to depend for the rest of our lives on energy that comes not from ourselves, but from the universe, nature, the angels, the high masters and teachers. You may call it Chi energy, Reiki, the blessings of the saints, of Mother Mary, of Jesus, the Buddha, or Shiva, etc., but one must tap into the spiritual wellspring that is available to us by means of the soul.

But to receive that energy, one must have a spiritual life and a practice. That is how we tune into the soul.

How else can you tap into the wellspring of the soul but through meditation, prayer, study, works of compassion and spiritual presence? Only after we have learned to not over give or overuse a profession and have developed a spiritual practice will we be able to continue working a profession in the world. One literally relies on spiritual energy from the Holy Ones, which is transformed into physical energy. This is spiritual alchemy. It is possible and it is powerful. Energy is transmitted from above and expressed through our human lives. It's real and it works! The change I am describing above can be huge for the person who has burnt out. The energy is there for anyone who invokes it. But the spiritual life has its own set of needs and values that one must live by. It demands a discipline, a way of life.

Some people tap into this sustaining spiritual energy by returning to church or a supportive group. Attending church can lead to deep soul-opening experiences where spiritual energy runs and flows beautifully. However, for others the experience of church attendance can be blinding to what soul and spiritual energy is all about. Sometimes it depends on who the preacher is, who the congregation is, the history of a congregation, or of an area of land and what has, and, or has not been dealt with in that location. Or, it may depend on the individual personality. Maybe church is not the setting through which they receive inspiration.

There are people who find a spiritual connection by being in nature, or with the practices of chi gong, or tai chi. For some people, these practices alone without a personal spiritual connection may not be enough. Nothing can replace the spiritual connection that comes through regular meditation, devotion and homage. Be aware that many people need a wholesome community and, or a spiritual guide, or counselor to change their lives and life patterns. Work with the soul never ends. Connecting with it is an enduring and rewarding commitment.

Rekindling a Connection with the Soul.

For anyone who works hard to not burn out, one must question what nourishes, heals, or refreshes the inner you. First and foremost, the soul is very interested in your relationship with the Divine. It is the Divine that nourishes, heals and refreshes us through the soul. Here is a list of ways that we encourage our relationship with soul to enhance the healing nourishing process. Perform these activities with love and care and you will find yourself in the realm of soul:

- Healthy relationships (relationships that nurture you)
- Writing or journaling
- Some type of compassionate action or practice
- A skill. What skill do you bring to the world? What is your profession? I believe that to do a profession well is to be in touch with the soul. This is especially so if that profession ultimately helps others in genuine ways.
- Art (painting, knitting, sewing, cooking, carving, architecture, etc.)
- Receiving the healing arts (acupuncture, acupressure, various forms of massage therapy, reiki etc.)
- Music (Always avoid music with foul language or negative themes.)
- Nature (being in nature)
- Exercise. If you have pent up energy, the best

way to help your soul is to release it. Sometimes before releasing pent up energy it is important to know what that energy is about and where it comes from. Exercise really helps balance body energies. We are highly influenced by worry, doubt, fear, sorrow, anger, and rage. Physical movement and activities release these from our body as they come up. A wholesome workout also balances our body metabolism so that access sugars in our bodies are used up appropriately and released along with stress and tension. Those who exercise regularly will lengthen not only their lives but also their quality of years.
- Meditation
- Yoga
- Wholesome food
- Spiritual study and reflection. Stimulating the mind with positive spiritual information and reflection allows the mind to resolve conflicts, and inspires our development. Human beings need a continuous influx of positive and wholesome information. This allows the soul to further awaken to its own immensity, its grandiosity.

What is most important is how you practice the above skills, gifts and talents.

If you practice them with intention, there is more reward than if you just do them.

The Dalai Lama says it's better to say (the mantra), "OM Mane Padme Hum," just one time with good heart and sincere meaning and prayer than to say one hundred with no intention but to get it over with. Quality is important, but quality requires attention, intention, and reflection.

Tibetan masters ask their students to meditate on the quality of good prayer. What does it look like and what might quality prayer even feel like? Likewise, the student is asked to meditate on what the qualities of a Buddha might be and what might those qualities feel like. The student is then suggested to stay with those feelings until ready to live them. One can do this because the Buddha essence is within you. Reflection on quality leads to essence. A Christian might ask what are the qualities of the soul or of living soulfully? Or, what are the qualities of Jesus Christ or of a saint. What are the qualities of a story or verse in the Bible? If a person can put the ego aside and meditate on what those qualities might feel like in your own body, then, through the imagination one becomes them. This is very much what "A Course in Miracles" is all about. These practices help one get to the essence of soul, and if you are devoted you will come to know Jesus as your beloved. If you can imagine or feel it, you can become it. One becomes like the stained-glass window with the light shining through.

When you take a verse from the Bible that presents the opposite of one of your bad habits and meditate on it, for a short period, with feeling, every day for six months you are causing a permanent quantum change within yourself. Cellular change happens when we meditate for positive change. This is referred to in Buddhist meditation techniques as "securing the antidote" for transformation and change. In Buddhist theory, this is how we can break karmic patterns. Buddhist monks take this stuff seriously. One observes with the imagination a felt desire, which becomes the quantum change, and it happens. All you need do is discover the negative patterns, the negative habits, the negative personas that you want to face and change. Next find an appropriate antidote, which is the opposite of what the negative habit or desire wants. It can be a story, a verse in sacred scripture, or the life habits of a saint. Then apply a felt visual image of yourself doing and being the positive actions that reflect the opposite of the negative habit. Meditate this way for at least six to ten minutes a day for six months and see what happens. My guess is that you will note a significant difference, and very possibly experience a quantum change!

You do not always have to focus on limiting bad habits to produce quantum change in your lives. Another way to stimulate change is to meditate on the positive virtues and qualities of Jesus or the Buddha. In this way, you initiate the good into your life. Focusing more on the good brings in good experiences. As one spiritual director told me, "You need to get beyond focusing on the negative parts of yourself by doing something that makes you and others happy." Likewise, you can observe yourself too much. It is not a good thing if you continuously focus on the experience of lack or just your negative qualities. Rather than focusing on your negative qualities might you want to focus more on your goals, or what makes you happy?

The whole idea of quantum physics is that we the observers influence the outcomes of scientific studies. In the same way we are also able to influence our personal lives and circumstances. We can do this through study about the goals we wish to happen in our lives, along with active meditation, use of the imagination, and desire. The book, *You 2*, by Price Pritchett, explains in very coherent language how to take an active role in the creation of YOU. You 2, allows the individual to challenge themselves to new horizons. To accept new directions that serve your desired goals, your authentic gifts and talents. One must be wise as to what one asks for and visualizes, as it just may happen.

In quantum spirituality, we work with and through Universal Laws. You will do well to begin by asking Spirit, "What is my true life calling?" When you are sure of either your first step toward becoming your true calling, or if you are absolutely sure what your calling is, then imagine yourself doing it, and being it. Visualize and feel yourself loving what you do. As described above, one aspires to become the essence and quality of that calling through meditation, desire, and study.

According to recent studies in psychology and in quantum physics what you expose your imagination to especially in regard to video games, movies, and music is what you become. Our psyche is highly influenced by what we orchestrate for it to receive. The movies that we watch, video games that we play, and meditations that we participate in engage the imagination. Even the ambiance that you choose to sit in informs your imagination. So, if you sit in a restaurant, at a concert, or in a bar you are exposing your psyche and soul to all that is playing out in front of you. Being selective about what you expose yourself to is important.

If you meditate on your kind and loving aspects, but then play video games where you are shooting and blowing up human beings, you are completely undoing your meditation. We are downloading whatever we expose ourselves to. If you like nature and watch documentaries about how to care for the natural world you will be more focused on nature and more compassionate toward nature. If you watch movies with lots of violence you will store anger energy to be used somewhere later on in your life. If that energy is not channeled consciously in a healthy manner it will creep up when least expected.

Here is a reflection I wrote on quantum physics and the law of attraction. The reflection suggests that we may want to have the intention to live consciously, through love, kindness, forgiveness and other virtues:

You are pure potential. The thoughts you choose to think, the words you use, how you treat yourself and others, how you care for yourself, that habits you create are the possibilities that you create for the future. This is in regard to yourself, your family, and those around you. It doesn't mean that unfortunate or bad things will not happen to you. But it does mean that people create the probability of how their life is going to be by their intentions and actions. So, what thoughts do you have about yourself and how do you treat yourself? Do you have health consciousness? How do you treat others? Do you forgive yourself and others? What words do you use when you communicate? What is the influence and vibration that exists around you? That vibration is you, it is your creation, and according to quantum physics what vibrates around you will most probably happen to you in return.

Chapter 2
Spiritual Presence

This section on spiritual presence comes from my training and experience as a hospice spiritual counselor, courses of study I received at JFK University in California, and computer research on Anapanasati meditation and various Tibetan Buddhist meditation techniques. I took graduate courses from PhD professors who taught counseling psychology; one using Eckhart Tolle's book *The Power of Now*, and another taught counseling psychology from a Buddhist perspective.

Through the art or discipline of being present, we make contact with the soul. The task of the soul is to help us experience life in its fullest, but this is not done or performed alone. We are part of and belong to the universe in all of its complexity. Soul is all about harmony and harmony requires being in relationship with all that is. The soul uses the imagination to teach us how to be in harmony. Creativity is important, but we can orchestrate devastating results if we create without harmony in mind. Without harmony, we can easily destroy ourselves. The soul is that part of ourselves that wants us to realize the importance of the interconnection of all things. These realizations come to us through being attentive, present, and still. The story below attests to what can happen when we offer nonjudgmental presence to another human being.

I sat with Jackie, a hospice patient, and listened to her on-going list of difficult life experiences. Jackie had a lot to process. She had the type of life I wouldn't wish onto anyone, was a good person who was met with many downfalls, and a lot of sadness. Jackie only wanted to be at peace with some of the dramas of her life before she died. I asked her the basic questions, what is your greatest fear? What is your greatest worry? What is most important to you right now? What are you willing to let go of that will make your life a little easier?

After an hour of being present with Jackie, something shifted. I had been listening to her many truly sorrowful stories and felt great pain with the revelation of her concerns. I continued to hold presence, to not judge Jackie or her experience, but rather focus on presence through attentive listening. Suddenly, a greater presence seemed to have entered the room. Jackie became aware of herself, her true self amidst all of her life struggles. The pain of her memories seemed to have lifted, and she began to cry. After a while I realized that she was crying tears of joy. "You don't get it," she said. "You didn't judge me, you heard my stories, and now I feel so accepted and loved just as I am." Jackie reprocessed every story that she had relayed to me from the light of not being judged by either herself or others. A greater intelligence had joined us in the session. The wisdom of this new presence helped me know what to say, and what questions to ask Jackie to help her look at her life. I actually heard what words to say to Jackie. Her tears freely flowed for another glorious hour. Jackie processed a great deal within a very short time. At the end of the session she acknowledged that for the very first time she felt free from the entrapments of her life.

Jackie got to work. The focus of her very sorrowful life was no longer the topic. She had become aware of her new work. "I'm dying," she said. "Now I need to reconnect with people and make amends, to ask forgiveness and tell them I love them, so I can leave this earth in peace." For the next three weeks Jackie spent hours on the phone. Soon after, people from all over the United States came to visit her. Many of her friends remarked, "What happened to Jackie, she is so full of joy and gratitude and yet she is dying." Many commented that Jackie suffered a difficult life. That she had been a vibrant person, but one day so much went wrong in her life and soon after Jackie had given up hope and friends. A month later, Jackie died with her friends and family at her bedside. Her death was a peaceful and beautiful event.

Through being spiritually present to Jackie, the doorway to her soul was opened and through that same gift of presence the wisdom that she needed flowed freely. There is a tremendous wisdom that comes with the soul. The soul wants us to acknowledge and experi-ence its grand intelligence. Presence is the doorway to the soul and the key to its wisdom. The soul's job is to bring us to the awareness of great mysteries and help us understand them, and for the mystics, to even become them. The soul's very duty is to help all of life to understand that there is a harmony between, though, and underneath all created things. As said before, the soul is the interconnection between these, and so desires to inspire us through creative interest to become living participants in what is or has been created in the universe.

For the mystic, the soul is that part of us that allows us to become one with the mysteries: To realize that ultimately, we are the mysteries. One realizes this in one's personal life experiences, through various meditations, and the use of the imagination. Mysticism is a life being attentive to soul. What sets the mystic aside from others is the fact that while the soul is present and available to everyone, the soul actually pursues the mystic.

What is Spiritual Presence?

Presence is the state of being without all the stuff that we attach to life. Spiritual presence happens when someone is aware of self or another without judgments. Being attentive to another without judgments, prejudices, or bias is love. Spiritual presence is exercising companionship with another or attending to another with focused attention and care. The practice of presence helps us live soulfully.

I enjoy being with people while in a space of the heart. I listen as they speak about their lives in matters of depth or concern. When I am present, something happens. As I become attentive with others, the sense of awareness increases, and a door of intuition comes through this gift of care and attention. Perhaps one could refer to the gift of presence as shared care and attention, because from that place we connect. I am learning that care and attention given together create something new. If a person is processing his or her life while I am attentively present it seems that new worlds emerge more easily. The person with whom I am being present feels safe and an energy arises that supports them to be able to look at deeper parts of themselves.

I was taught by one of the professors at The Acupressure Institute in Berkeley California that when I am present to another person in an interview, or when performing acupressure, the soul is activated. This allows the person I am with to also engage the soul as well. The soul is part of the Divine, therefore, healing power is present. The soul is especially active if the practitioner has compassion for the person, and even more so if the technician of acupressure and the client are both actively seeking consciousness through meditation, Chi Gong, or one of the martial healing arts. During counseling sessions people have expressed to me that they have felt safe and experience shows that they tend to share deeply, or they just enjoy the moment of being.

Sometimes, the person I am listening to with presence and attention begins to cry for no apparent reason. Often, it is during these times the client, or person being listened to, brings up a great loss that has not been safely looked at. Presence and attention allow whatever topic needs to surface in its right time. While being spiritually present, there is no hurry or worry or rush about processing a particular topic.

Presence as Invitation

When a person is with another who is spiritually present, there is an automatic invitation to join the spiritually present person in that place of presence. In the state of presence, there is no need for worry, doubt, sorrow, fear, anger or rage, because in our authentic state none of those things exist unless we entertain them with the mind. To have presence of mind means to have stillness of mind. Therefore, it is in the state of presence that we can safely look at the emotions of worry, doubt, sorrow, fear, anger, rage, or, share any profoundly good memory, belief, or poem.

In my experience as a spiritual counselor, I have learned that there are many memories and sacred utterances that people want to share but have no one to safely pursue their desire to do so.

A safe way to learn how to be present with others is to learn how to be present to yourself. Sit in a quiet place of nature and just be aware of yourself and how you feel at this time. You might want to jot how you are feeling in your journal. After you have taken time to carefully articulate how you feel in the present moment, again, be present to yourself. Just sit with loving attention with yourself. Carefully and with care, observe yourself. Observe your breath and how breathing flows through your body. Be aware of what you are sensing in your ambiance. Taking it in and letting it go through breath. Have no judgment, just be. At any moment, a message may come from your inner-self that wants to be expressed. This is a good way to do reflective writing. Most of this book was written through this form of reflective presence.

The Practice of Presence

The practice of presence is not just for spiritual counselors and attentive listeners. It is a healthy practice for everyone. Actually, it is necessary for consciousness to unfold. Eckhart Tolle teaches about the practice of "presence" or being in the "now moment." The greatest practice is surrendering to the moment of what is. One allows things to come and go without placing attention on them.

Another way to put it is that you become the observer. One cannot observe without being present. This is a strong Buddhist practice. There are Buddhist texts that speak of being able to observe not only what one experiences in the present moment but to also observe the one within you that is observing. If you can observe the observer, you have reached a high state. Yet it is so simple. Within you is the observer who observes everything. If you can observe the observer within you, you have located a divine place within yourself. The observer is one's own highest Self, which is of course one's Buddha nature. Christians might call it their Christ nature or Christ Mind. Hence, if you are truly present the observer is involved and therefore the Divine is accessible. Anything can happen if in the presence of a true practitioner of consciousness, presence, and meditation. The Dalai Lama admits that he performs spiritual practices five hours a day to keep his spiritual nature intact.

The Journey of the Soul

Through stillness and presence, we begin to realize that within us is a watcher, a witness, a greater mind. By observing the watcher, you will become the watcher. If a person continues with the spiritual practice of meditation and listening presence she begins to see and feel, to witness, that she is being protected by this greater mind. Over time the greater Mind, and the greater spiritual guides become active participants in the incumbent's life. Hence, behind all thinking, behind the clamoring of the human mind, is a protector, the True Thinker, the Universal Mind, the Life Force. This True Thinker awakens the practitioner to a change of consciousness. With time and practice, thought eventually becomes more easily directed. Debris from the past is healed and left behind, and dualistic thought is stifled. Over time the practitioner learns through active imagination and willpower to direct thought in ways that heal, protect, and maintain both spiritual and temporal goals. Along the way, the creative aspects of the individual begin to surface desiring expression through poetry and art. Creative expression becomes a means through which one communicates to the world, to the Divine, and to one's self.

Through listening presence, or stillness, one becomes aware that all things have consciousness. Eventually, the world we are in becomes a synchronous melody through which we live and move and have our being. Silent communion with what is reveals our true selves to us. This can be a most humbling experience, while at the same time an introduction to our own sublime gifts. Yet be warned, sometimes the gifts we have, our true purpose for being on this planet are what we fear most.

Bringing It Deeper Through Meditation

The daily practice of meditation, Chi Gong, Tai Chi, etc., becomes a home to focused learning. Through medi-tation one can learn about other worlds, as insights from other cultures and religions may open up to you. As part of your spiritual growth process, you might be called to experience these other cultures and their religions directly or from within. While in medi-tation you may find that you actually communicate with adepts from other parts of the world. The practice of the stillness of the mind often goes beyond personal and cultural limitations. This is because through the soul we are intimately connected to all other beings on this planet. Through meditation and still presence there may come a time that the worlds of the angels, high spiritual adepts, even Buddha's, connect with you.

With the practice of meditation, the energy centers of the body called chakras will open, and many influences will want to come in to ride the energies. Some of these may be negative influences. Some positive and negative influences will disguise themselves. This can be a con-fusing and even dangerous time if the initiate is not aware and if he or she does not have wholesome spir-itual direction for guidance. Some of the disturbances may be from your own history or from the ego. Other influences come from outside forces. One must never lose heart but rather call upon the protection of Christ, Mary, the Archangels, Masters, or Buddha, who may have introduced themselves during meditation and prayer. After having called upon the Great Ones, be silent in the face of the negative forces. Silence transforms evil because it has no way to influence the mind.

If you silently observe the presence of the antics of something negative, it loses its force. This is why having a counselor to share your life struggle with can be so important. If the counselor listens with present attention and non-judgment, the client is free to see himself or herself for who they are authentically. They are given a window to see clearly that beyond judgments and emotions they are a unique and beautiful person. In our authenticity we do not carry these burdens. They no longer have control over your mind and lose their grip on you. The most important thing is to not let a negative entity engage your mind. Sometimes they like to come in through your emotions. That is another one of its games.

I have learned that many of the lower spiritual energies are looking for someone to help them rise out of their situations. My spiritual friends call them members of the lower astral planes. They play games just for fun, or they genuinely want energy so they can influence things for themselves. They often use trickery to get what they want. I have had images of my deceased mother come tell me things that just were not quite right. I knew it wasn't my mother. It just didn't quite look like her. The message was for me to include someone in my prayers. I saw an image of that person which was also not quite right. It was suggested that I send that image love and peace. The message left me perplexed and disconnected from my present moment with prayer. It was a false message.

Yet, I have had impressions from my mother and other relatives from the other side, and I felt and recognized their love. The message was an invitation, or an acknowledgment that they were with me to support me. The sense of presence and peace pervaded. Their presence added to the experience of elevation and happiness. Obviously, they were relating through the soul. To this day, I can remember the feeling of love and presence I felt in that moment of visitation. That was an authentic impression from the spirit world.

We have the opportunity to call for spiritual help from the Masters, Archangels, or Buddha, on a daily basis for protection and guidance. We are living in times when much has been stirred up. Do not wait for negative things to happen before you call upon the guidance that is there for you. Calling upon protective forces is a daily discipline. However, sometimes the more light you have, the more the not so friendly forces will want a piece of the action. My Native American friends often taught that if you have a lot of light that there are people and spirits who will want to steal some of that light. Some will do what they can to take it. But they cannot take it unless they can convince you to step down toward their level of existence. In other words, they wait for you to step out of the light. This is why wild sexual fantasies or thoughts of anger, blame, or self-doubt seem to come from out of nowhere. The medicine man Armando stated that sometimes these are residues that come from our own lives, other times these thoughts are introduced to us by crafty bystanders from the lower astral plane. As soon as your heart sinks with guilt, shame, fear, anger, or desires, you have become vulnerable and energy that you worked hard for can be lost.

I am often awakened at night by presences passing through. Sometimes people who are genuinely asking for help awaken me. After years of suffering I learned to call upon the Archangels and Masters for help and then do focused meditation accompanied by the intention and petitions that I have a peaceful night. People have often wondered why I go to bed so early. If I do not make time to pray before I go to sleep, I rarely have a peaceful night. If I drink alcohol, I cannot go into that place of contemplation before resting to the pillow. Alcohol seems to open all the windows and doors letting just about anything in. I imagine drugs would do the same. By inviting in the Spiritual Masters, occurren-ces at night have greatly calmed and become manageable. This awareness has come through hard lessons. A known spiritual practice for initiates is to read spiritually uplifting material for ten to twenty minutes before reclining, thus granting a peaceful night. This is true, it helps.

Once you are sure and clear in your daily protection, you will find that overcoming negative energies allows a new energy, a new spiritual force to emerge within you. But this new energy must be nurtured and cared for with changes in your lifestyle and diet. As the chakras are strengthened and opened, the body will change, and its needs will change. Temptations toward addictions may completely fall away. Addictions live in the lower chakras of need, want, desire and greed. If you dwell on a regular basis in the higher chakras the voice of addictions becomes silent. This is why Alcoholics call on a Higher Power. Distractions to the spiritual life either fall away or are able to be dealt with. Meditation, yoga, works of compassion, and study of spiritual topics are the best avenues for opening and dwelling in the higher chakras.

As a person rises in awareness and consciousness, he or she may become sensitive to genetically modified food or become allergic to chemicals. Many become sensitive to noise and violence. People who have become more spiritually aware often need to resort to homeopathic or other natural remedies for health. This is because some healing methods or medicines in general do not feel healthy anymore. One lives as the body tells you to live. One lives as the small still voice in your heart instructs and guides. This is all part of the soul's journey. We need to be present to all parts of ourselves, our bodies, our psyches, the environment in which we live, and our daily spiritual encounters.

If your spiritual centers are opening be kind to yourself. Practice stillness, consciousness, yoga, and healthy diets, as the body desires. Spend time in pure places of nature. You may find that you will want to limit the activities of your lifestyle to mostly your calling and your practice. The extras fall away. A new center will begin to emerge within you that has always been there, but, was not awakened. This is the wisdom center of your own true heart. Your own true heart is loving, invulnerable, tranquil, and vast because it is attached to a universal spiritual center, the soul. Ask to be taken there, once in that place one sees from the other side and duality is no more. All along the way the meditator is occasionally taken to that tranquil, timeless, formless place. But to remain there is a miracle.

Stepping Out of Chaos into Peace

Often times when we feel that energy has turned chaotic, it becomes a lesson in learning inner peace. The question then is, what establishes inner peace? Notice that we are focusing on the inner peace and not the inner or outer chaos. While choosing to not allow chaos to be the main focus of your life you must, however, be informed as to what is going on in the world. Otherwise you will not be a balanced person. Even though we are doing our best to not be part of chaotic energies, we still live here in the midst of it. We are human beings on this planet.

I myself do not listen to the news on the television. I do not even have a TV. It would be too much stimulation if I did that on a daily basis. I use the computer to breeze through the headlines. But usually the headlines are where I stop. However, on occasion I read an article just so that I know what is going on in the world. I have a few social justice minded Facebook friends who also keep me up to date with new events. About once a week I go to Barnes & Noble and check out the magazines and newspapers. That is enough for me. It is all part of keeping myself informed and grounded. I am sure there is a lot I'm missing out on. But, for peace of mind, I have learned my limit for exposure to bad news.

More often than not it will be very difficult to experience deep self-reflection and personal growth while exposing yourself to negativity. Recently, I attended a talk by Lama Kathy Wesley. She participated in a three-year retreat to become a Tibetan lama. While on retreat, family members were encouraged to not write letters about their problems nor about the atrocities happening in the world. The retreat was designed for study and learning, deep reflection and meditation, and therefore expansion of consciousness. Lama Kathy warns that too much exposure to negative news and worldly activities holds one back from growth in consciousness. Reflective presence is necessary for personal wholeness. Lama Kathy took a three-year plus three months, plus three weeks, and three days retreat from exposure to the world's toxicity to achieve growth in consciousness. She relates that she is a much better person for having done so.

This brings us back to the original question: How does one establish inner peace? You and I must have moments of quiet. How much is a moment? That depends on the individual. Some people might say that a moment is five minutes, but that is not enough to create a healthy psyche. In today's society most people need at least one full hour of silence or quiet time a day. For myself, I perform best with two hours of quiet time. This means no cell phones, no TV, no loud or fast music. Frankly, I'm alone and quiet.

You might ask, what does one do during those hours? I Meditate, reflect, pray, write, just be, study by reading spiritual information, or walk alone in nature. In other words, I am being present to the world and myself. This helps me find my place in the world. It helps me to know who I am.

Besides quiet time, I also need enjoyment time. I like going out to dinner, or to have tea with a wholesome friend. I enjoy walking in nature with a friend or friends. Reading is a great enjoyment for me. I like nature documentaries, and science and history documentaries. These keep me up to date and informed about our world. I eat good wholesome food and exercise regularly. Intimate moments are important. I enjoy taking time every day with my partner to discuss where we are at with each other. We discuss the many topics of our lives. We respect each other's personal space but also spend time together in shared presence. We love the arts.

The combination of wholesome activities of personal and shared presence brings me to inner peace. All the above activities are life balancing and allow for self-nurture. If I participate in these practical life habits on a regular basis, I find peace much easier than if I do not practice them. This for me is soulful living.

But there are certain things I must not do as well. I do not go to noisy places with loud or offensive people or music. I do not wake up to the news. I wake up to at least one hour of quiet and meditation. I do not watch anything that is violent or that stirs my sexual/sensual desires. If I do, I get caught in these things. At age sixty-five sexual and sensual desires have taken on a different emphasis, and a deeper meaning, than when I was in my twenties.

Being present to our authentic selves means limiting ourselves from certain activities. We limit who our friends are going to be and expand who we want our friends to be. This is very important. If you are like me, you'd rather be alone than be disappointed. It's all about the phrase "know thyself." But to know what is best for you is an invitation to act. I have friends who participate in long rigorous hikes almost every weekend. Others take to their boats and or go fishing. What matters is, what works for you? I know some people that if they are not surrounded by family members every day, most of the day, they feel lost. That is their world, but I cannot be who they are. Their identification with what brings peace will be different from mine. If you know yourself you will know what is good for you, with appropriate action, you can know inner peace. Inner peace is all about forming healthy habits. It takes time and effort! If you like and enjoy having people around you all the time, just remember that there is nothing wrong with good company. But if you are impinging on other people's time and space for your personal comfort something is wrong. If you are afraid to be alone, there is more than likely an emotion, an experience, or a deep pondering question that needs to be looked at and addressed.

Calming Emotions

When I was in seminary in the 1970's, I learned from a wonderful Catholic priest, Eric Kahn, how to calm my emotions. He suggested I sit still with my back straight in a quiet place. Then I was to focus on my breath for at least 50 or more breaths. He noted that my mind was going to wander but to simply, without being in thoughts of frustration, to simply gently return to focus on the breath. The idea is to refocus on the breath without giving much thought to thought. I have found this exercise most helpful for calming my emotions. Not surprisingly, Tibetan and Indian yogis practice this same technique to calm emotions.

Focusing on the breath is an ancient Buddhist form of meditation. But it has been an ancient Christian technique as well. It was and still is used by Christians when praying the Jesus Prayer, a prayer of the Desert Fathers and Mothers. As one inhales one says silently and with love, "Lord Jesus Christ." On this inhale you may also gently visualize that you are breathing the light of Christ in. On the exhale, one says, "Son of the Living God," breathing redemption, love, and compassion out to the world. There are various phrases that are used to perform this meditation. One can focus on the breath by visualizing the light of Christ coming into yourself and going out of yourself, or, as a feeling of love coming in on the inhale and love being sent out with the exhale. All of these exercises work well. Each has a different effect on the psyche. If a person has doubts, the prayer can be said with an emphasis on faith and belief in the Master Jesus. If a person suffers from anger the focus would be on the emotion of love received from the Master and then given out to the world; the very world that he has redeemed. Supported by the Master, one participates in the blessings and powers of the Master.

There are different and longer versions of the Jesus Prayer, but all of them involve the same technique of using focus and breath. The focus is gentle, not stern. This prayer is most powerful for developing a personal relationship with the Master. It is the exact technique used by the yogis of India and Tibet to come closer to a deity or the Buddha.

Taming Entities

Sometimes the meditator or initiate is more sensitive and experiences disturbing entities, spirits, or disruptive feelings and emotions. This is a normal occurrence. A good method that helps tame entities and feelings is focused mediation for one hour a day. This hour of focus can be done in increments and actually it is recommended that one does so. Then each period of meditation is not so intense and is apt to be more clearly focused. Visualize an object of choice that is pleasant to you such as a rose, an icon, the Buddha, Mother Mary, or Quan Yin. One can begin with three five-minute sessions and increase them gradually to 20 minutes each session. For many people 20 minutes for the whole day is enough. But if you are dealing with disturbing entities the sessions of focused meditation need to add up to a full hour. Again, this is not intense focus but merely bringing one's attention back to the image of choice. Try to stay with one image.

If a person is devoted to having a daily practice of meditation, he or she will become much more aware of self and others. This is a natural process of consciousness. Awareness leads one to a higher state or personality within. This personality or wisdom within relates to all beings on whichever level of spirituality he or she is dwelling at the time. The Hindu call these chakras or energy levels within the body. One communicates to the universe out of the chakra level from which one abides. Likewise, one invites into the communication forum from the level you have chosen to dwell. It is like the rising spheres of Dante's trilogy, (in which sphere do you want to dwell?). They go higher and higher until one comes to elevated levels of consciousness, infinite glory, the home of the Masters, the Buddha, the Christ, Heaven.

But let us not be fooled, as the opening of some chakras may take years. Teaching, as you may know, is about the throat chakra. I love teaching, but it took me years of training to get there. I had to attend classes, write papers, and teach part of the courses taken during my graduate studies program. All of this, plus a disciplined spiritual life and practice has enabled me to currently hold the title professor and be able to teach. All along the way, I have had to be present to myself and others to develop and expand my various chakras. Presence allows for integration.

Purity vs. Impurity

Eventually, you will find that to ascend on the spiritual journey there is a need for purity. Why? There are certain high beings that cannot come close to you if you are impure. Sensitive people end up carrying what we expose ourselves to. Even good movies we watch, or just watching people at a mall, can affect us depending on who or what we encounter in the movie or at the mall. I know people who are even affected by what may have happened in places a long time ago. Some people are naturally born sensitive. Sensitive and especially spiritually sensitive people pick up the energies of people and places that they are exposed to.

In about 1985, I visited my brother in northwestern Georgia. I knew nothing about that area. My brother asked me to come with him to a worksite. As he drove, I fell into what seemed like a stupor. I sensed that terrible things happened in that place. I saw many dead bodies and heard screams of pain associated with battle. I felt nauseous and told my brother that something horrible had happened here. He immediately apologized stating he did not know I was so sensitive. We were driving through the Chickamauga battlefield where tens of thousands of Confederate and Union soldiers died. I know many people who are sensitive to events of the past, and it took me some days to get over the experience.

But impurity has to do with more than just being sensitive. For many people, impurity has to do with confronting bad habits and addictions. Whatever your addictions are, that is your impurity. Many of us can afford to drink less alcohol and eat a healthier diet. Many of us could use a better exercise routine. Some of us could gossip less. Certainly, who we spend time with also has an effect on our wellbeing.

However, if you do imbibe in something decadent, be wary of judging yourself. Try not to be harsh with yourself. Being spiritually present and honest about what you did has far more benefit than causing a lot of guilt. We are human, and all of us learn by trial and error. However, if you have a nagging continuous action that holds you back from growing consciously, then you may have to take deeper action. Speak about your concern, be it an addiction or not with a spiritual director or counselor. Observe, or be present to that part of yourself that lures you into the action or the desire behind the action. Then learn what caused the need to entertain the desire. Usually, there is a hurt lingering behind the need that causes a desire for escape. Study it well as it may be a key to your growth and freedom. Notice that being nonjudgmentally present to yourself helps you go deeper into the topic at hand especially if there is a significantly present person with you to help you explore the situation at hand. A spiritually present person can help cause powerful realizations and healings. Presence provides safe ways and means to get to and explore the core lingering pain in our lives. There is much to be said for having a positive, trusted, witness to help us go through difficult experiences.

My psychologist friends have often noted that couples going through a divorce go to the wrong friends for reassurance and counseling. This usually causes them to experience more sorrow than they need to. A lot of people want to resolve situations with or from a negative approach. They give bad advice. They believe that because they have been through a divorce that they are the professionals about divorce. The last thing a couple contemplating separation or divorce need is to have outside negative influences. They need positive non-biased observers who have care in mind.

I have friends who have seriously dated but dropped

their partners because they did not want to look at themselves and the negative traits that they bring to the relationship. Every conversation I had with them was a continual hype of complaints about the faults of their boyfriend or girlfriend. Sometimes I felt that their partners were wonderful potential partners. Those who struggle with relationships need others around them who give loving and wise counsel. There is nothing wrong with letting go of someone with whom it's not going to work. But the source of a solution or a block to a happy relationship could rest in either one of the partners, their relatives and friends, or counselors. Anytime a relative, a friend, or a counselor are emotionally involved or have an emotional charge about a situation, they should step back from trying to help resolve the solution for the couple. This is because what they bring to the situation is not pure.

Purity has to do with the conscious mind and who or what we consciously choose to be exposed to. This means who, what, where, and when. We are the directors of our lives and need to make choices that reflect our desire to be in the right company. To the degree that we ourselves see clearly is to the degree that we will see what is happening in our lives. We also will see who is best for us to be around during a conflict. What has helped me see myself clearly is having a friend to talk to about my life and circumstances plus have time and place to be present to myself. Presence is very cleansing.

I have found that when I keep myself and my relationships pure that the angels, the spiritual master's and teachers, and other higher spiritual guides show up in my dreams and prayers. To the degree that we can companion a master teacher for a while allows us to learn deeper spiritual and even mystical concepts. Hence, purity demands that we be the captains of our ship. We need to make choices as to what waters we course through and with whom.

For most of us, before we make communication with spiritual guides, we will do well to find true teachers who are in our midst. Often this will come through a rabbi, minister, priest, public speaker or an inspirational writer. Educating ourselves is pertinent to spiritual growth. Having an education through instruction, by whatever means allows stimulation for continued growth.

But for many of us, purity goes beyond trained professionals and spiritual instructors. It may involve what we eat and drink. Wholesome food is necessary to have a wholesome body and is necessary for spiritual ascension. Spiritual ascension is merely higher consciousness. There may be times that you have a calling to eat less meat or even become a vegetarian. Over the past ten years, Tibetan high lamas have taught that one does well to consider becoming vegetarian. They also teach that care of the environment is significant for our times. These practices of loving-kindness bring purity. Anything that we do to help the present and future generations allows for the earth to remain pure and intact as a living agent to support life. This is important. What you do to the earth, you do to everyone. What you do to others, you do to yourself. What you do to yourself, you ultimately do to the whole planet. Being conscious of what we eat, how we treat the earth, and who we spend time with, are part of being spiritually present.

Adding Presence to Your Daily Life

I had been praying for inspiration for my book, the

topic being spiritual presence. I received inspiration in an unusual but immediate response. Walking out the door to go to work, I realized that I had forgotten my keys. But the keys were nowhere to be found. Let's make this a very short story and say that it was a very tense day. My partner lent me his car so I could go to work. But on my return home and having looked everywhere, I finally just gave up and gave it up to the Divine to take care of things for me. Giving a situation to the Divine is the first stage of letting go. This means not to worry about it as it is in heavens hands. This moved me immediately into the second stage.

The second stage began when something inside me said to just be present and not lose my happiness about the fact that I was not able to locate my keys. Note that I did not say that I had lost my keys. I knew not to affirm that they were lost. The moment I became present an intuition came to me and I remembered a game that we used to play as teenagers on the farm. At that moment, I recalled in my mind's eye what the keys looked like and focused on that image. I then walked directly to where the keys were located. They had fallen off the key rack and lay hidden behind a toaster oven.

Ironically, in the game that my sisters and brothers used to play as youngsters, we used an old-fashioned spoon that had a design on its handle. A chosen person and two helpers were to gaze at the image of the design on the handle of the spoon. One of the three was then taken out of the room, and the spoon was hidden somewhere in the room. The person outside of the room was then blindfolded and returned to the room. The two helpers stood on either side of the blindfolded person and held his or her pulse on either side. All three then concentrated on the design on the spoon with the intention of the blindfolded person finding it while blindfolded. It was a miraculous game as sometimes the blindfolded person walked right into the direction where the spoon was and grabbed it. Sometimes this happened even when the spoon was behind an object. Other times, the blindfolded person walked directly into the direction where the spoon was located and was really close to it. But because the object was too well hidden could not find it. Sometimes concentration just wasn't there enough for the miracle to happen. All in all, this was a fun game.

Literally within less than a minute when I decided to stop worrying and become present about the keys, they were found. The game from my past having flashed through my mind led me to the key. This is how miracles work! Often, it's a matter of getting me out of the way. I was given an immediate answer to my prayers not only about the keys but also about seeking inspiration about spiritual presence. To receive inspiration, all one need do is ask. But in this case, for a couple of hours I was about to lose my bearings. I was judging myself, and feeling a bit beaten up by my ego. My partner stated after he had given me the keys to his car, "Now I have no car." I wanted to react thinking that he was criticizing me. My emotions were stirring, so I had to ask him, "Are you trying to make me feel bad that you've had to lend me your car because I cannot find the keys to mine?" He stated, "No not at all. I'm merely stating a fact." At this point of clarity, I was able to just let go of the accusations of the mind against my partner and myself. Only then was I able to come to presence. It was a still small voice within that suggested to me to just let go. I followed it and presence came. I learned a lot about spiritual presence and what one has to give up to get there. But take note, spiritual presence led me to take an action. I was to visualize what the keys looked like and trust. Only then did I find them. Take note that both presence and the imagination were involved in the miracle of finding my keys.

Presence and Intention

Presence reveals what needs to be known in the moment. This is especially so if one has prayed about something with intent and released it to the Divine. This is also true when you are with another person and have the intent to help them. Spiritual presence demands that there are no judgments, not even against yourself. There is just presence with the object in one's heart and mind. In the case of another, the other is held with love, care, and attentive listening for the sake of that person. Spiritual presence is a powerful miraculous tool. What is needed in the moment will come to fore.

If one has the intention to be truly present when counseling or with a friend, whatever topic comes up will have a deeper dimension. The counselor will be able to see further into the truth of what is going on with the client. Be aware that being present often requires an action or an intention. One holds presence out of compassion for the person in front of them or one visualizes an outcome. There is a science to this.

Communications professors state that as 80 percent of communication is nonverbal. The nonverbal aspect is tapped into when someone or both client and counselor are being present. Presence reveals what is being referred to that is not being verbalized. The ability to understand body language and intuitions seem to be heightened for the intended purpose at hand. Presence reveals what is being said that is unconscious. Presence often reveals what someone is trying to say when they do not have the vocabulary to say what they want to say. Presence also reveals what the deeper meaning of a topic is. It reveals what has significance in the life of the seeker. The person being present with the client is at times given a glimpse of what and how the emotion or imagination of the other is contemplating. Deep insights can be revealed. I believe that this is how scientists will be allowed to further their knowledge and forge new paths for our future.

Presence and the Imagination

It is good to ask; *How does the soul utilize the imagination?* What is the imagination? Webster defines it as the "faculty or action of forming new ideas, images, or concepts of objects present or not present to the senses." It also is described as "the ability to be creative or resourceful." It even works with the fancy, or fantasy of the mind, if you will.

Most certainly the imagination is about what interests you, what fascinates you, what gives you passion. The imagination is telling of what you are curious about or afraid of. If there was one thing that your spirit guides, the masters, and the angels want to do, it is to stimulate your imagination. Without you becoming curious and creative, there is no growth. It is apt to say that if you have no curiosity or sense of being creative then your imagination has shut down. But as in the game that my brothers and sisters played in the past, imagination was key to setting things in motion for a desired goal.

A suitable way to grow spiritually is to watch what it is that the universe tries to teach us. A person does not have to believe in a Divinity, or the angels, or guides of any kind to realize that at every moment the universe is continuously both collectively and personally instructing. The imagination is deeply connected to what the universe tries to teach us. Because of the law of harmony, the entire universe is teaching at any given moment in time. We are always being instructed. We are never alone.

The imagination is a vehicle of the soul. If you are having a moment where you are free of your habits and addictions, what comes instinctively to the imagination is usually the action of the soul. We participate with the life of the soul when we use our imagination. The soul responds to whatever situation you expose yourself to. The soul is interested in what you are interested in so that it can inspire you to work with the greater harmony. The soul's main duty is to help us realize that there is a great intelligent expanse available for us to relate to. Beyond all of our conditioning habits and addictions our normal state is to relate through the soul. We relate to this great expanse through the powers of the imagination. The imagination is one of the main vehicles of the soul, and the soul is one of the vehicles of the Divine. You may refer to the Divine as God, Source, That, Infinite Intelligence, The Mind of Light, or The Creation. Whatever it is, it is That which orders all things.

When I was studying at Catholic Theological Union in Chicago, one of my professors offered a course in Lakota Rituals and Spirituality. I took the course to find that study of the Lakota myths and rituals opened up an entirely new world for me. I was left in awe and was pulled by and through the experience of awe to live with the Lakota people in the summer of 1984. A tremendous energy supported me for this journey.

While in South Dakota, I lived on the Oglala and Pine Ridge Reservations. The local people, medicine men, and Jesuit Catholic priests all encouraged me to do a Vision Quest. The advice I received to prepare for the Quest was to awaken every day before the sun rose and visualize the rays of the sun surrounding me and flowing into me. I was to take long walks on the prairie away from people and listen intently to every creature – even insects, the grass, and stones that surrounded me. This demanded attentive presence. I was asked to visualize the energy of the Earth coming up through my body. Each time I did these meditations with the sun and the Earth, I was to petition earnestly and with humility that a vision would be provided when I performed the Quest.

I will not relay here what my vision was but want to portray that use of the imagination through visualization, focused attention, and humility are the keys to life beyond what we consider reality. These keys allow one to relate to the soul that ministers to us when we are ready. One needs to have a true desire to be of service to receive a vision. Without the correct attitude, the soul may just pass you by and wait for another time. To receive a vision is a reception of power. To give power to a person who will not use it wisely could be a dangerous mistake and the cause great harm. The soul knows when someone is ready to receive their vision. A vision quest is performed for service, never for selfish gain.

Here I repeat the message about soul from the beginning of this chapter. The soul wants us to get to know about and acknowledge that a grand intelligence exists, and it shows us how to participate in it. The soul wants us to know that its job is to bring us to the awareness of the great mysteries and help us understand them, be in harmony with them, and for the mystics even become them. The soul's very duty is to help all of life understand that there is harmony between and behind all created things. As said before, the soul is the interconnection between these, and desires to inspire us through creative interest to become living participants in what is or has been created in the universe. For the mystic, the soul is that part of us that allows us to become one with the mysteries: To realize that ultimately, we are the mysteries. One realizes this in one's personal life through various meditations, humility, study, and the use of the imagination.

I personally believe that in one lifetime or another we will all eventually become mystics. After a few lifetimes of being a mystic, we will work with the mysteries directly, through the imagination, the use of a trained mind, and accompanying actions. That is what the great Sadhus and Yogi's do. If you think about it, this method of using the imagination to find lost objects or yet undiscovered solutions to problems is similar to the methods used by Tibetans to find their newly incarnated Dalai Lamas, Karmapas, and Tulkus. Those searching for the object of their desire remember the deceased leaders' qualities, virtues, and authority of office. Holding these in heart and mind they begin their search. The very people who were deep followers, and those who loved the person being sought are the very ones sent to search for the new incarnation. Once again, love and devotion go a long way, even to discovering miracles. These methods are tested over time. In the same way Hindu and Tibetan Buddhist methods for divination are received through training. Investigations are tested from the wealth of experience. They have made a science of divination. The diviner must be truly dedicated, with a trained mind through use of the imagination, and above all, they must be virtuous. The imagination empowered with love, determination, and zeal brings the fruits of reward and discovery.

Through the imagination we have the gifts of creativity, vision, inspiration, inventiveness, resourcefulness, ingenuity, originality, and innovation. Through the imagination we express interest, are fascinated, are attentive, passionate, and curious (paraphrased, Webster's Dictionary). Without these, there is no growth, either personally or collectively.

One of the best ways to engage the imagination is through storytelling. We are, after all, telling ourselves stories all throughout our lives. The stories we tell ourselves are what we believe, and our actions support our beliefs. It is important, therefore, who or what we believe in and what we expose ourselves to. Having a positive heart and mind is also important. When we expose children to wholesome stories they are stimulated into new worlds of opportunity. Stories stimulate growth, either positive or negative.

Storytellers are aware that stories exude a presence. The audience may be struck with deep emotion, whether positive or negative. Each story has a particular feeling attached to it. How the feeling is received depends on the listener and the emphasis that the storyteller places onto the story. Stories help us to live in a shared world and there is much to perceive about our world. Stories instruct us. They tell us that what stops our awareness of a shared world is selfishness in the forms of vanity, pride, arrogance, greed, desire for power, and competition. These are the unfortunate lessons of what living in a shared universe is all about. Stories remind us that we are meant to be in harmony with all beings. The imagination is one of our greatest teachers. It opens us to the learning process. It touches our senses, which ignite uniquely in the body of each sentient being an awaking of information for the purpose of learning, participating, and understanding. The imagination brings worlds alive, including the world we live in, through intuition and storytelling. Though we live in this world, through story-telling other worlds are evoked or brought into being.

Through story, we role-play the images of our thoughts and create what we have imagined. In other words, through the creative powers of imagination and story, new worlds are created and can be participated in, thus the reality of this world is explained or expanded. Imagine for a moment how the world was when we did not have cell phones or computers. We invent worlds and bring them into our shared world, our shared experience.

Another important aspect about story is that it touches each individual uniquely. I like to tell a story to an audience and then allow the audience to be present with the story for a while. For some the story will have a feel to it that affects the listener. For others, the story seems to explain or resolve something to them about life. For another, the story recalls memories or hopes and dreams. The list goes on. When presence and story are put together every person is affected by the story from where they are at in their life. Then they are allowed to present themselves to the depth that they want to go with it. The next time they hear the same story, they may feel tempted to go even deeper with its meaning in their lives. Or, the story may reveal another whole side of itself to the listener. True storytelling is non-threatening, yet, stories can issue stern warnings. Whatever the story, the listener seems to take in the meaning more rapidly if they stay present with the story for a while and then feel free to discuss from their own life experience how the story is affecting them.

A story that is not pulled apart by moral, psychological, or intricate explanations or diagnosis serves everyone in the audience. The same is true of story that is not influenced by dogma. When dogma interprets the story for us, we are not free to experience the story for ourselves because it is already interpreted. The individual's imagination is shut down. This is a hierarchical or a fundamentalist's model. It is far better that human beings have a healthy balance between interpretation and experience. In indigenous communities, the grandparents are both the tellers and the interpreters of story. Their main duty is to uphold the values of the culture. When I heard Indigenous Americans tell stories there was always a still silence among the listeners. Only sometimes was storytelling followed by instruction. Storytelling is a highly effective model for teaching.

The Dark Imagination

The imagination can be used for good or evil. When we are angry, many atrocious things come to mind. All of our moods affect the imaginative process. Buddhists believe that when we give the power of our thoughts and imagination over to negative purposes we may have to live one or more lifetimes where these things actually happen. This is why the imagination needs to be connected to the workings of the soul. All human beings need to take care of themselves. Human beings need appropriate rest, exercise, friendships, food, and accompanying thoughts. If you are an immoral person, you are part of the dark side of the imagination. This happens when what we create is destructive and ruled by negativity. Furthermore, all human beings need to take care of other human beings. What you do to yourself you do to others.

Likewise, if we are lazy and do not use or discipline our imagination, the imagination can use us in negative ways. Further, if you do not use the imagination the ego will. It will give you suggestions (through words and images), as to why you can slack off while at work. It can trick you into being more materialistic by sending you unnecessarily off shopping. It may suggest that you stop what you are doing and have a drink or two or take up smoking again. The imagination is a vehicle that operates of its own accord if not harnessed. How dangerous is that if we do not have a set of morals in place?

Through the imagination we visualize our future. Many people who are in prison had imagined themselves performing the crimes that they eventually got caught at. Some people who commit suicide imagine themselves doing it over and over again before performing the act. The imagination is an incredible tool meant for learning and growth, but it can be used to perform terrible actions. Being that we have the power of free will we can hone and train the imagination for our own betterment. This is best performed through focused meditation, the practice of awareness, and being present. Through meditation and visualization, we can recreate our thoughts and lives and come to know peace. Meditation is a method of stilling the mind. One is then not controlled by the mind. Again, this is because when the mind is still the observer within us is able to guide us. Visualization is a means of utilizing the mind to create new results in one's life. Guided meditations can be very powerful because what is negative can be transformed into something positive. Excess and frustrated energies can be transformed and utilized for an intended outcome.

From Darkness to Light

Have you ever had one of those periods of time where you feel that life is very difficult? Perhaps grief after death feels too much for you. Death often leaves us with deep unresolved questions. That is how I felt after a brother of mine committed suicide. To help myself along, I kept repeating to myself often throughout the day, "God, please make something good of this." Eventually, I found that I could not function and sought out a professional counselor. My Jungian analyst assisted me through active imagination to relieve the stress and pain I felt at the time. She helped me to go into meditative journeys wherein that which was negative in me was explored and dealt with safely. Active imagination is a form of meditation wherein someone is directed to transform access and negative energy into positive energy. This is a highly potent form of self-discovery and allows for a lot of healing in just a few sessions. Never go on such a journey without calling upon Christ, Archangel Michael, the Buddha, or some other arch-protector. Who you have as your counselor or depth psychologist does make a difference. With active imagination we literally journey to the other side and allow the psyche or soul to re-imprint difficult interpretations of life into positive interpretations of life. It is un-storying the self on a deep psychological level.

The therapist must be totally present to the client and to the soul's message. Each person's experience and story is unique and active imagination allows the individual to tell his or her story and express their feelings without harm to themselves or another. Sometimes the deepest hurts are revealed and healed, other times experiences of joy permeate the session. Active imagination is a form of alchemical change. Its effects can be profound if one allows the soul to lead the way.

After my experience of active imagination from therapy sessions, I decided to have training in the art of active imagination. I have had numerous people come forward with great pain who found resolve through active imagination. Deep transformation occurs. One must trust the soul wholeheartedly to lead and guide the session. Most people who came to me lost a loved one and needed the experience re-identified. In nearly all the sessions a bright light appeared to them or a guru or spiritual master showed up. These are all images of the higher self. In the sessions I allowed the client to dialogue with the higher self, which is a direct connection to the soul. One must be present to the soul and its action within the client. Each time, clients came up with unanswered questions from within themselves. In most sessions I've facilitated a deep healing or realization occurred.

While studying the process of active imagination, I learned very quickly that the best way to end a session without the healing effects was for me to give mental interpretations to the symbols or the story of the client that arose during the session. That is because human interpretations can be short sighted and incomplete. It remains a question as to just how much a symbol ought to be interpreted, as they speak for themselves. The mind is a wonderful instrument, but it cannot take the place of the intuitive flow of symbols. Symbols are archetypal images which originate beyond thought. A mental diagnosis may cause the flow of energy to stop, and the client may go home without satisfaction. One must allow the psyche, another name for the soul, to guide the process of active imagination. Nonjudgmental presence is key to this process.

Getting in Touch with Peace

Getting in touch with that place of peace within is something that I work hard for. Internal peace is a treasured gift that I find happens sometimes only a few moments a day if and when I'm lucky. But it makes all the difference in the world. Because of that gift, I am able to do the work I do as a hospice chaplain, counseling the dying, their families and caregivers. Over time, I have learned that the gift of peace comes from present stillness. I cannot take credit for being an instrument of peace except that I do show up for my daily meditation practice and I do call upon the Divine Masters, teachers, and protectors to help with the process. Then I ask them to help me get out of the way so that they can do their work.

Increasing the Light

I have also learned that as one's light grows so does one's spiritual knowledge, opening the way to more experiences. There was a time when my spiritual practice, and dreams became quite powerful. I was being led on journeys. At times, I felt accompanied by beautiful or powerful beings. Some were very friendly and helpful, and others were not. My spiritual director immediately suggested the use of spiritual guides for protection. I learned to call upon my own personal guide, the Master Jesus, and my guardian angel, as well as the archangels. These have been my friends ever since. There have been harrowing times where I have called upon the saints and angels only to find immediate assistance. They are real and quick to respond. But the only way to maintain a relationship with them is to keep the spiritual energy going. One must meet these beings where they are. So, a spiritual discipline to rise to higher levels became pertinent and part of my normal daily practice. But going to higher levels of spiritual awareness isn't enough. Beyond going just vertical we must also grow horizontally in our spiritual journey.

Human beings are communal by nature. We do not do well without other human beings around. Even mystics and contemplatives who isolate themselves step out of isolation to commiserate. They share their earned wisdom. This brings sanity to their experience. Contemplatives are sometimes far more involved in the things going on in the world than we who are enmeshed in it. They are enmeshed from a spiritual perspective. I had a couple of Poor Clare nuns who prayed for me on a daily basis. I had not seen one of them for about two years and then when the opportunity for us to meet arrived I was given an enormous amount of information about myself that she provided. The nun, Sister Margarita, informed me about what I was going through, when I was going through it, and how she had to pray to help me through it. She even knew my sins. But when she revealed these things to me it was as if I was being informed by a best friend who deeply loved me. I then understood the feelings I had of someone helping me. I felt no sense of shame for my mistakes but only edification to serve all the better. This came from a woman who was deeply entrenched in the higher Light of Christ. She saw herself as a vehicle, or vessel, for the workings of the Divine Order. If we are connected to the Higher beings of Light, our ability to help each other is limitless. Provided, of course, if the person wants to be helped.

Sister Margarita spends time every day in deep meditation. She calls it being present with God. Ironically when she revealed to me what she knew about me, I felt the Divine Presence was present to me. This is the gift of spiritual presence.

Spiritual Nourishment

I learned from one of my spiritual directors that the spiritual life demands a need for spiritual food. This meant learning and making time for spiritual reading. When I was a member of a religious community, the reading of the scared scriptures was a daily, continuous event. But to locate other appropriate spiritual wisdom, became important as well. Our soul, on the personal level, is in constant need of new information. It is constantly learning and growing as well as experiencing. It does not like to lay back and relax for long periods of time. It likes to be active. The soul realizes that this is a lifetime, and it should not be wasted. At the same time, we live in modern times, and the soul wants to be updated as to what is going on around us. What gadgets we use and how to use them is important. There are new scientific discoveries flooding across the planet at this time. We need to know the basics of what is going on. It is not enough to be just and only interested in the spiritualties of mystics past and church documents. The soul longs for the new and wants to be part of the new that is coming in and onto the planet. Therefore, current reading material, experience, and reflection as food for spiritual growth and thought is important for the aspirant. As long as we are in this human body, our soul will lead us on to greater wisdom and continuous growth.

Compassion and Service

Compassion and Service are very important aspects of the soul's yearning. Without service, there is no community. Without service, there is no practice of what one has learned while in meditation, or out in the world. The soul needs to practice while manifesting in the physical world. Spiritual energy needs to be grounded. There are many ways that one can manifest. Within our service to the community lies the gift of self-discovery. Through compassion and service, we learn what our authentic gifts and talents are and how to use them. Beyond using them, I have learned that the soul is picky. It not only wants us to use our gifts and talents, but it wants us to hone them. It wants us to become specialists at some things. This often means that the student needs a profession. A profession is the means for us to demonstrate our gifts in the world. It is also our source of gratification. It grounds one's identity giving a sense of accomplishment and purpose. Being in the world and rubbing shoulders with human beings is what allows for the balance between what is above and what is below. Heaven and earth unite through the service and compassion of a human being. My work as a spiritual counselor for the dying often leads me to get out of my own small problems and focus more on what others are going through. Interestingly enough, when I do that my problems seem to disappear. Getting out of my own way allows me to be present to others. Then compassion and focused action come through. This is wholeness. This is what it means to manifest.

A Review: What is Spiritual Presence?

All too often when I mention the words spiritual presence people look at me, with big eyes, like a deer staring at auto headlights in the nighttime. As a hospice chaplain, spiritual presence is commonly applied, but the general public, including some healthcare workers throughout the strata of health care, do not understand what is meant by spiritual presence. Many people do understand what it means to be "present." But to add the word "spiritual" to it leaves some people in a questioning daze.

To be present to another is to be available and, as much as possible, without judgment, prejudice, or bias. In the moment of presence, one holds space for the other as well as holds space for healthy boundaries for self and other. This is an expression of love and care. It is referred to as sacred space if presence is held with the intent to be of service to another. Being present to another or holding sacred space for another can be a tangibly gratifying experience for the parent, nurse, social worker, spiritual counselor, or therapeutic counselor involved. The experience of loving-kindness is usually a gratifying experience.

My friend Camille surprised me when she informed me that she had secrets. I immediately held attentive non-judgmental presence with my friend. What sort of secrets? I asked. The conversation went deeper when Camille shared with me that she is a recovering alcoholic of many years. But as we discussed, I learned that Camille had yet other secrets. She began speaking of having nightmares about a family member. I asked what her relationship with that family member was like, and she shared with me that this family member is deceased, but that it was an abusive relationship. I asked her to tell me the dream and it was clear that the particular family member who was deceased was reaching out to her through a dream. Camille then asked, "Well what does he want?" Due to the nature of the dream I noted that this family member was asking for forgiveness. Camille, who is a very spiritual woman replied, "Well, if there is one thing that I have enjoyed and hold as my deepest kept secret it is that I will never ever forgive certain family members." She even admitted that she has taken great pride in not forgiving. I then referred back to the dream and to health issues happening in Camille's life. In the dream, her deceased relative was even offering to help her if she could just forgive. Camille had shared deeply and was taken aback by this offer. But the next day she called me by phone and asked how to do it. "How do you forgive someone that you hate?" Again, I held spiritual presence with my friend as she relayed her painful story of the past. Then she asked to meet in person.

This time, Camille noted that when I listened to her with such attentiveness it felt like love, and she felt drawn to share more of herself. She noted that since she had shared the dream and listened to my comments about it, her life was turning over with a whole new realization. That day, Camille wrote a letter of forgiveness to her deceased relative and she asked forgiveness in return. Then she burnt the letter, sending it to heaven. Within three days Camille noticed that muscles that were always tense across her back were releasing and felt flexible. I encouraged her to help the process by getting a massage and considering yoga. Within six months, Camille's life had completely changed. This is because her relationship to her deceased relatives had changed, which affected how she treated herself. Camille had a new, happier life.

When a spiritual counselor companions someone on a journey through life's questions, they are present to that person. What is presence? I find that presence is going to that place within myself where I am available to my own or another's needs and values. I also locate presence within myself when I remain in that place where the Divine seems to enter or show itself. That for me, is a spiritual ambiance within myself, when I place myself in the space of presence, and attention. While in presence, I am aware of the individual. I am aware of the life story that they have shared. I am aware of the words they choose and the tone of voice that comes with their words. I am aware of their body language. Because I have had counseling training, I also am aware of my own boundaries and needs when I go into a session. But while being aware of all those things in the back of my mind, I am not focusing on them unless I need to. Rather, I am present to an individual when I am with that person in a nonjudgmental safe environment. I create that safe environment as much as possible. A person needs to feel free to express their deepest self that wants to come up at the time. Or perhaps they do not desire to share anything, yet I remain comfortable in the present moment and remain present to the person.

To be present, one does not pry unless the situation or a need requires it. Hence, presence involves, companioning an individual. It is a means to allow the world of the other to be expressed as authentically as possible.

My own biases and thoughts of or about a situation need to be put aside as much as possible unless in a moment it will truly help the individual I am with. This method also can be applied to families or groups of people. Whatever discussion arises from the patient, or client, or friend is what is discussed. It is a powerful experience when hearts meet. When the hearts of a spiritual counselor and a client meet, the spiritual counselor may want to ask inviting questions that allow the patient or family members to share deeper. Or, just remain in that moment of hearts meeting. The therapist or spiritual counselor is not afraid to be compassionate. At the same time, the therapist or spiritual counselor does not get enmeshed in another's business. Spiritual values are tapped into when counselors are exercising presence.

Be aware, however, that many business people and sales persons also hold presence. They are attentive and affirming, some of them even baring judgments. But their ultimate intention is to make a sale. Their care for the person may not be very great. You will notice how these people tend to walk away from you as soon as they realize that you are not going to be a productive sale for them. It is about them. On a rare occasion, you will meet a sales person or a business person who also cares about you.

To hold a spiritual moment means to desire the very best for another in that moment, or, to connect with the Divine Source in a moment for the sake of self or another. Spiritual presence then, is about accessing the Divine Source, or consciousness, so that it may flow through. Or, said in another way, it is about learning the application of the Divine Source in the moment. From the Divine Source, "presence," you will know and learn much more as it comes to you. One is available to the Divine while present and allows It to be in charge as needed. Presence usually opens the gate of intuition.

One must use discretion when, where, and with whom to open oneself to Divine Presence. While in that state, one can be vulnerable if a daily practice of meditation and prayers are not in place. But once safely open, there is a deep strength that accompanies it. It has potential to surprise anyone and everyone because wisdom seeps through. It can be used as a power to advise, offer words of comfort, and heal. It can even surprise one with a gentle or firm correction. The initiate will experience the performance of Divine Presence as It activates through his or her own soul.

But take a warning, to behold such a grace and power, the beholder's personality will be affected and change. Likewise, over time, one's opinions of oneself, and of others, will change. As the incumbent observes the gift of Divine Presence flowing through them, he or she will relax around people and they will relax too. Once a relaxed state has been reached, in a natural way more people will come just to be close to the person with the gift, to hear what they have to say. When you learn that you carry the gift, be sure to spend time with those in need, and the weary. They will so appreciate you for taking the time.

An Encouragement

All of us who care for others as parents, teachers, spiritual counselors, or therapists need to take care to watch over ourselves. Never release yourself from the grip of happiness and loving-kindness, as these will always support you. More than that, because of happiness and loving-kindness you'll be able to express yourself more fully and thoroughly.

Ways to Practice Spiritual Presence

There are ways to practice "presence" or "spiritual presence." These exercises are simple and easy to follow. Also, spiritual presence is not ever forced. It is an invitation to be present to or with someone. If someone does not like it, or want it, you do not offer it:

One) Obtain a blooming flower plant or a plant of your liking. Sit in a quiet place and observe how beautiful the plant is and then send it love. You may even tell it that it is beautiful. This is a simple five to ten to fifteen-minute exercise. I performed this exercise with an orchid. Its large white flowers were strikingly beautiful. To my great surprise, the following day, the plant clearly spoke to me.

Two) While you are walking feel the earth beneath your feet. As you continue to walk, slow the pace down a little and with each step take notice that you feel the earth with every step. After a while send love to the earth from each foot upon impact with mother earth. More than once while performing this exercise I found myself awakening from a trance. This exercise is best performed in a place of nature and takes about 20 minutes time.

Three) Sit comfortably in a chair and pay attention to your breath counting them up to number twenty-five, or forty, or even more. This is a great exercise to perform if you are angry or fearful. It takes energy away from the anger or other emotions and returns it to your psyche allowing you be present to what is essential in the moment. The Dalai Lama states that if you want to grow in serenity that daily meditation on the in and out flow of one's breath is the key. One needs to count above one hundred breaths for serenity to develop. Many Tibetan mystics count up to one thousand breaths in their daily practice.

Four) When you are with a friend, be especially attentive to what he or she is saying. This is a very good exercise to assist students of counseling.

Five) While walking in nature be especially attentive to smells, textures, light, color, movement, etc. I've done the same when I had a cup of rich aromatic coffee in a French bakery. This exercise reduces stress quite efficiently.

Six) The more you become present, the more you will realize that the world we live in is an illusion. Therefore, one must ask the question, who is the real you? Only by developing the quality of being present with observation will you eventually realize who is the real you.

Seven) Exercises that will help you learn who the real you are comes about by gazing intently upon a flower, an image of Christ, or the image of the Lord Buddha, etc. After doing this for a while, then observe the one who is observing.

Eight) The way you are, and who you are is a presence in the world. The fact is you are here, and you are influencing the world around you. Part of the vocation of the Catholic and Orthodox religious orders as well as the various sects of Buddhist monks and nuns is to be a presence in the world. This is the same with monks and nuns the world over, even if they are cloistered. If you do not understand how a cloistered monk or nun is a presence in the world, you do not understand the soul.

Chapter 3
The Alchemy of Soul

What is Alchemy, and How it Applies to Our Lives?

This chapter is about the transformation or alchemy of soul. Alchemy is a seemingly magical process of transformation. The soul is that part of us that allows us to transform, to experience life and Divinity. It is about expansion of, and growth in consciousness. Much of human expansion is due to thought and how we use our thoughts. Alchemy is all about having the right perspective or thought or even no-thought (as in non-judgment or presence) on a particular subject. Studying and observing thought provides wisdom and growth. Presence and non-judgment hold tensions without trying to influence their outcomes. Very often this brings one beyond duality into a third thing. Something new comes to surface. This is the alchemy of life. Alchemy is the gold of our efforts wherein we have moved beyond our struggles into peace, into greater consciousness, into wholeness.

Likewise, our thoughts, hopes and dreams, and all that we imagine influence our future. Hence, the probability of what we experience or create is shaped by our thoughts and imagination. A quantum leap is as much a transformation, or transmutation, from one substance or situation to another as is alchemy. This is the basis for quantum physics, and we live quantum lives. As human beings we observe and participate in everything just by living life. Our observation, our participation, our meditation and thoughts affect the outcome. Hence, alchemy and quantum physics are related.

The fact that an individual as observer influences the outcome of an experiment has been tested over and over again. But what about group consciousness, where the invisible stuff (thoughts, hopes, dreams, and imaginings) of everyone is collected, collated, and brought back to them in the form of physical results? What are we as a group creating? According to some Buddhists nothing is allowed that has not first been met with approval on the collective level. There is such a thing as collective karma. I attended a retreat wherein Tibetan Buddhist Khenpo Karthar Rimpoche stated that President Donald Trump could not have been elected to office if there were not at least 51% of the country in agreement with his general trend of thinking. This is collective thought. The outcome of the election experiment was influenced by the desires of the collective. One could argue that he lost the presidency by three million votes, but millions did not vote. The outcome reflects the theory of quantum physics. Khenpo Karthar implied that whatever the lessons that this country, the United States of America, is going to have to learn over the next few years are the lessons associated with this president. That is karmic law. This means that in the moment when the thought of the general population tipped to the 51%, for better or for worse, there was a quantum leap into a new future for this country. It was an alchemical change from the Obama era to the Trump era. Thoughts matter and lifestyles are thoughts lived. This means that we must be careful about what we believe in and what we do while on this Earth.

Through thought and action, we humans have the

potential of alchemical power. The question is, are we willing to make that quantum leap to shape our thoughts and actions so that they reflect harmony with all human beings on the planet? Many religions believe that producing harmony is the duty of human beings. However, if one looks at our history evidence shows that humanity is slow to learn.

The Law of Interdependence

One can easily see and feel opposing differences between people by the thoughts or opinions they hold. This felt sense is even more so when it comes down to the differences between political parties. But what about the unifying factors between people? Buddhists do not believe in an individual soul. But if there is such a thing as a collective soul, the below quote from the Karmapa offers a representation of what its purpose is all about. The Gyalwang Karmapa, Ogyen Trinley Dorje states: "We should not feel like we are strangers to each other but rather that we share a collective karma with one another on this earth and it is our responsibility to try to improve it. The basis of Lord Buddha's teachings is that nothing rises by itself and we are not individual entities living by ourselves. The law of cause and effect and interdependence should encourage us to develop compassion for all living beings on this planet and for the earth itself. One beneficial act can have a multiple number of positive effects. We should feel greatly encouraged and determined to protect nature for this reason." (HH The 17th Karma; source: kagyuoffice.org/his-holiness-the-karmapa-speaks-on-.../)

Another example of the interdependency that we are all meant to live comes from the Dalai Lama. A friend of mine attended a gathering of about 7000 individuals who came together in a stadium to hear His Holiness the Dalai Lama speak. Someone asked the Dalai Lama just how many lifetimes it takes to become enlightened. The Dalai Lama explained that every individual present in that stadium had been a brother or sister with every other person there present at least one lifetime, and with some individuals they had been siblings or married etc., up to as many as twenty times. Hence, enlightenment takes a long time unless one is consciously working to become it. He also noted that before incarnation we all know each other very well and we are sent here to get along and work for a better world because we are all brothers and sisters. This means that there is a collective urgency to bring peace on this planet. This urgency, however, is not felt or known unless we dwell within the higher levels of consciousness.

The Matrix of the Soul

When I reflect on my life's experience and the Dalai Lama's comments about how interconnected we really are, the thought comes to mind again that the soul is a hologram of which we are all a part. We belong to a matrix. What happens to one part of the matrix happens to the whole of it. We all come from the same Source and are made of the same Light.

The ego gives us a mistaken sense that we are separate individuals. But in reality, we are totally interdependent. The ego would have us believe that our experience is our own as an individual. It even pushes toward individuality and competition. On another level, the ego tells us that we are part of a particular tribe, society, or religion, and others do not share our language or skin color.

We are even told that we are separate from nature

and that we ought to subdue it, claim it, and own it. But in the true reality, nature is as much a part of the hologram as we are. It just does not have the same mobility and though processes that we have. Indigenous people believe that we are here to be in harmony with nature, and we have been endowed by the Creator to take care of the Earth. We are meant to work with nature for the betterment of all beings. In actuality, you and I are one and the same, more interdependent than we'd ever want to admit. Here is a poem by Rumi interpreted by Ravi Kopra:

> Joyous, blissful moment, sitting on the porch, you and I
> two forms, two faces, yet one soul, you and I
> The groves' gift, the birds' songs give us the water for ever-
> lasting life, when we come to the garden together, you and I
> The stars of the night sky witness us
> we show them the moon together, you and I
> You and I united as one in ecstasy and delight
> Cast aside absurd stories and nonsense, you and I
> The parrots of the sky eat sugar when we are
> on the veranda, laughing together, you and I
> How amazing are we here this moment in this corner
> yet we are also together in Iraq and Khorasan, you and I
> We are in one form on earth and in another in the
> Everlasting land of honey – the paradise, you and I

This poem reflects Rumi's friendship with his teacher. They were not lovers but one in mystical union. Together they had embraced the Highest Light. But the nature of his poem is timeless and therefore the poem is meant for all beings. Rumi taught from the experiences of his life. But being that his consciousness had an elevated perspective, what he wrote is relevant for all beings. The above poem can reflect any person's mystical union through love. The poem itself is transformative.

A Journey Into the Highest Light

Tibetan Buddhism speaks of a light called The Mind of Clear Light. This light is composed of compassion, generosity, morality, wisdom, purity, truth, and love. It is the Highest Light and has no evil in it. In Buddhist thought we go into or diffuse into that Light when we die. This same Light can be experienced in moments during meditation or prayer, etc. Only the highest enlightened beings can remain there. For further review, see the Dalai Lama's book which prepares one for death and rebirth. The Dalai Lama and Jeffrey Hopkins, Mind of Clear Light, Chapter 8, "The Clear Light of Death." New York, Atria Books. 159-181.

I am a Christian, yet one day I prayed to the God beyond all gods, beyond all thought, beyond all forms, and the Buddha presented himself to me in a vision. I have since learned that this Light is the same as the Christ Light. There is no difference. They come from the same source. It is likewise the guiding Light the Sufi's speak of. The mystic teachings of Sufism encourage one to go beyond the four directions of planet Earth to infinity. One does this by going within to the city of Qaf and then beyond to an inner spiritual dwelling place. When I encounter this Light, or hunger for this Light, I often proclaim, "God, I am One with God," or "God and I are One." We need to go beyond duality, beyond religion and culture to the eighth, ninth, and tenth chakras (the body's energy centers) to encounter spiritual alchemy. Once there we experience that God is One, and harmony is everywhere, in everything. Love and compassion are the basic normal living of how life is meant to be. This is the authentic self, a hologram. It is alchemical wisdom. Any wisdom that brings one beyond duality is transformative and therefore alchemical.

The Soul is Holographic

The Earth is home to many cultures and religions, but the collective soul does not separate human beings from each other. Mother Teresa used to say that when she was with another person she was with Christ. She understood what it meant to see to the deepest part of another human being. All are Christ. The soul is a hologram and so is the human being for all of us contain that hologram in its totality within us. Recall Rumi, "You are not a drop in the ocean, you are the en-tire ocean in a drop." This quote is a reference to the unified, collective, holographic soul of which we are all a part.

The only thing that separates us is the mind or ego. Religions are prone to have doctrines, and these tend to separate us. This is the opposite of transformation. The Divine does not separate us. Our beliefs define our limitations. If you are a believing member of a particular religion, you operate within the confines of that particular religions beliefs and doctrine. This makes it difficult for a person to traverse religious lines of belief. For the fundamentalist, the tendency is to become myopic.

But the soul is not confined to any particular belief. Rather, it serves the Infinite Source. The soul is intimately connected to the individual, relating the events of one's life to the universe and vice versa. From the eyes of the soul, religions, spiritualties, and scientific beliefs are paradigms. What paradigms are you as an individual choosing to work with at this time in your life? But we human beings are not static and often change one paradigm for another. May I suggest that you look into the idea of the paradigm of a uniting, col-lective, holographic soul? But be warned, if you choose to think about a collective soul through the eyes of a doctrine, you cannot and will not be able to even con-ceive the idea or essence of a collective, uniting, and holographic soul, unless you have a virtuous relation-ship with the Divine. The virtues of love and compass-ion have no boundaries. Beyond all religions, we are one soul.

Paradigms

Paradigms are models, patterns, examples, standards, prototypes, templates, or archetypes that we live by. Every religion models and teaches desired paradigms for living and believing. In the long run, only the highest paradigms serve us because they allow for transform-ation.

What happens when someone becomes disillusioned with a particular religion or paradigm? This puts a person in a place of questioning. A healthy religion allows its members to ask questions while remaining in that particular faith. The individual soul is then free to explore. This means that there is flexibility and the possibility of change within a religion while belonging to it. A stagnant or fundamentalist religion does not allow for questions or the free use of the imagination. These religions restrict and restrain their members. The imagination then is forced into the unconscious. Living unconsciously is never wise, for from there will surface old patterns that seek to be dealt with that one does not deal with consciously. From there one gives birth to secrets, guilt, and sin, perhaps even violence. One is held prisoner by these unresolved beliefs or patterns. Unless a person for some reason agrees to be held in a psychic prison, they will begin to question their need for freedom. This is where many members of a church simply stop attending. They say they still belong, but some part of them feels held back from what they authentically believe within. This would represent about fifty percent of the United States population. They claim a particular church of origin but do not attend. They refer to themselves as "spiritual, not religious."

But if a person is allowed to ask questions within the structure of their religion of choice, there is room for growth and development without leaving it. That is the sign of a healthy religion. However, sometimes there are people who question, dream, and imagine beyond their own religion and possibly even their culture. As a student and priest, I was a missionary and encountered a great desire to experience what was beyond the confines of my own religion and culture. I was led by a deep desire within to know and understand the Divine beyond the confines of my own religion and culture since as long as I can remember. This is a soul experience, and I was led to these experiences by the soul. It was not a personal soul that led me down this path but a collective soul, the collective soul that we all belong to. Ultimately, there is no division.

Liminality

But what happens to a person who traverses beyond his or her own culture and religion? I have known many missionaries, foreigners, and migrants who crossed boarders into other countries. These men and women all experienced a tremendous psychological change by having let go of their culture of origin. All that used to support them, all that they were used to was taken away, because in their new country things were different. If you go outside your religion and culture into the area of another religion and culture you more than likely experience that you belong nowhere and everywhere. You will experience the "space between," called "liminality." This is not an easy place to be at first. But eventually it may become home; the only home you feel comfortable with. Many artists, mystics, foreigners, and missionaries live there. These are the people who are free to ask questions that take one beyond boundaries. The liminal personality has experienced the psychological dimensions of alchemy. That is why they can be and dwell comfortably in the midst of other religions and cultures.

Liminality is not for everyone. It can be a difficult place to be because one's own culture and religion no longer support you as in the past. The experience can place an individual in psychological trauma. Once you cross the boundary of no culture you are subject to experience the powers of any culture you come in contact with. The stimulation can be overwhelming, powerful, and even beautiful.

Liminality is the place that shaman are brought to during their dangerous quests. Some do not make it out alive or sane. Surely, one will never be the same. Once there, you are marked forever, for you have touched the gate that leads to the infinite. Not everyone stays at that gateway. Many return quickly to their past and their own religion. Some cling to the old beliefs, all the more shutting down what might be for them a fearful adventure. The psyche only can handle so much, so some are wise to return. But this being the Age of Aquarius, many more than usual are going to have to take this difficult but necessary journey into the no-return that leads to new understandings, new awareness, and new intelligence, or even a mystic life. Behind this alluring power is the call to sisterhood and brotherhood that beckons us all: It the collective holographic soul. It has been well noted that missionaries often become bridges and healers between cultures.

Often times the journey is not a choice. Some of us become terribly ill, are in an accident or have a powerful vision or dream that cracks us open to the core, and we are never the same. The same can happen when a wealthy person comes face to face with a person who lives in dire poverty and opposites converge. One is no longer separate from the poor they had avoided. The experience becomes greater if you have to depend on them to survive. Then you have to conform to welcome that which sustains you. You will never be the same. Nothing seals the crossing of borders quicker than becoming a true friend or lover with someone who belongs to a culture or religion that is wholly other than your own. This is because love does not have borders.

We all need and seek love, but it is right underneath our noses. It's all around us, within us. Soul is connected with the infinite, which is love. Love and the Divine are aspects of the same thing, but they cannot be defined. They can be experienced but not defined. So, if while you live in another culture, and you learn to love people there, you have crossed into liminal territory. A transformation has occurred. You have crossed a border and from then on, as with love, many things are possible. You will see the world you came from differently. You may not fit in so much anymore. You may even feel adverse to where and what you came from if you feel at home in the new. This borders mystical territory. For many the only way to become part of the foreign culture is to become involved in it. If you see your place in another culture from the point of view of the virtues, it will go much easier for you. The virtues by nature are cross-cultural and go beyond all religions to higher consciousness. They in fact point to our only home, the soul. This is where Jesus, the masters, and the saints dwell.

Here are some questions to ponder:

What if heaven is not a place? What if heaven is simply immersion into higher consciousness? If that is so, then why wait till you die?

Soul Messages from a Lakota Symbol

During my theology training in 1984, I went on an immersion experience to the reservations of South Dakota. While with the Lakota I had a vision. I was deeply meditating, saying the name of Jesus with love and attention and suddenly experienced the vision. I was saying with love the name of Jesus throughout the vision. In this conscious awake state, I saw a sacred symbol, a Medicine Wheel, was presented to me. The vision lasted a long time. The medicine wheel presented itself as a person, a living loving being, though it was a symbol. I felt unworthy, and not until the fourth time that the symbol presented itself to me did I accepted it (and the responsibility that comes with it). The wheel that was given to me is a circle within a circle within a circle. I was instructed by Medicine men that Wakon

Tanka, Christ, and the Buddha dwell in the center of that wheel. I was told that any true being of love and compassion is there in the center.

While the center is within us, it is also outside of us. The entire symbol is both within and without. It depends on how one is seeing. Within the macrocosm is the microcosm and within the microcosm is the entire macrocosm. Within these is a way of seeing and much wisdom can be gained. The symbol itself is a sphere of the earth and its surroundings. The medicine man said, "This symbol is you. It is also the Earth and the Four Directions." Then he went on to say, "It is also a symbol of the entire universe." The Medicine Wheel is a hologram. The ability to see through and learn from the various dimensions of the symbol is alchemical insight.

The only way to ground the symbol is to live here on the earth with other human beings and be a person of love and compassion. Then the symbol reveals its power. Alchemy, like everything is practical. It is a shift with a practical purpose, which is consciousness. Consciousness is not just pie in the sky thoughts. It is grounded awareness utilized while among other beings.

Practical Alchemy

Many rituals are alchemical in nature. Rituals bring concerns of the Earth to a higher consciousness, or a higher chakra. One such alchemical ritual is to write a letter to Spirit, God, the Divine, the Master Jesus, Lord Ganesh, the Lord Buddha, the Mother Mary, or Quan Yin (However you address the Divine). I usually write a letter when there is something of significance or urgency that needs attention. In this letter you may ask a question, or make affirmations for protection and abundance, etc. When you finish your letter, which is written in affirming positive terms, you make your prayer to the Angel of fire to please bring this letter immediately to heaven. Then burn the letter. If your letter is in union with Divine harmony, you will get a quick response provided you are doing your spiritual work and you are seeking the Divine will as was requested in the letter. The letter written with your own hands comes from your heart and the efforts of your spiritual practice and prayers. That message is therefore infused with the feelings and concerns of your heart and will. The ingredients that make any ritual work are that the intentions of the heart and will are united with Divine will and formerly requested. In the above case, the letter is committed to fire thus transforming it and its message into ether. A soulful part of you has been brought to a higher level. It is a spiritual transformation brought about by uniting the desires of your heart with the intention of union with Spirit. This is alchemy.

Once burned the letter has become smoke or air, releasing the message into the ethers. Ether or space is a higher vibration, which is closer to Spirit in vertical spirituality. When you learn how to pray at the level of ether you can manifest on Earth, the horizontal plane.

Redirecting Spiritual Energy

Humans are able to redirect spiritual energy. I wish to recall here an instruction that I received from a medicine man, Armando Hernandez. "If you receive instructions or warnings about a phenomenon or something dangerous about to happen or that did happen through intuition, a vision, or dream you must respond to the situation that is shown to you through a spiritual outlet, such as prayer, meditation, or, visualization. For instance, if one receives an intuition or vision that someone is killed or injured by a certain person, it would not be wise to go to the police. You will be held suspect. To the mind of the police, how would you have known of the incident otherwise?" The medicine man instructed that one should go within, call upon one's spirit guides and then review the vision. Usually a vision can be changed if while in a meditative state you send a lot of pure white light with love into the situation until one feels that the circumstances have shifted, changed, or been healed. But one must do this while in a pure state with the assistance of the angels and higher guides. Often this prevents the severity of a situation or state of affairs from happening. Or, the visualization assists the situation so that the one who has committed the crime is caught. The same is with visions of storms or earthquakes, one does well to call upon the divine and visualize through light that the damage is lessened, and people and animals are kept from harm. These instructions are clearly spelled out in books by Agnes Sanford, particularly in her books, <u>Sealed Orders</u> and <u>The Healing Gifts of the Spirit</u>.

Creating a Stupa

I recently became interested in Indian and Tibetan stupas. For a period of time I was not getting sleep at night. Spirits and voices interrupted my meditation, prayer, and sleep time. Earlier in the year 2017, during a meditation, I heard what felt like a voice from Spirit say to me, "If you want protection build a stupa. It is highly protective." I knew that this voice was not like the others as I was in a deep spiritual state at the time. I was pondering the thought of protection from a stupa and was wondering how to build such a physical structure with all the correct prayers. I looked online and found that there are very specific measures one has to undertake to build a stupa.

To come back to my point, I was told through a clear message to build a stupa for protection. Hence, I came to realize that this meant I was to build a visual or spiritual stupa. I began by studying the structure of the stupa, its significance, and it's symbology. Through study I learned that the stupa is an image of the path toward enlightenment. Hence, after study of the stupa and its meaning, I began by visualizing the base, seeing in my mind's eye a yellow square representing the earth. Then I personalized it and said to myself, "I am the yellow earth." I held this image for about a minute thinking and feeling that I am grounded, strong, and solid, as all sides are equal in a square. This image brings in the concept or wisdom of equality and equanimity.

Next, I visualized that I was a blue sphere on top of the yellow square. I was still the square of the base, but I was also the sphere of water. I stated to myself, "I am the blue sphere of water resting on the yellow earth." Water reflects, and I saw myself as being fluid and at the same time having the quality of the mirror (deep inner reflection). Then, I visualized that I was a red pyramid above the water. I performed the statement, "I am the discriminating mind symbolized by the red pyramid of fire." This represents the active focused mind. After that I saw myself become the green bowl-shaped parasol of wind or movement. I stated, "I am the green parasol representing the force that moves. I rest above the red pyramid of fire." The parasol represents the forces of loving kindness and compassion. For these virtues have a powerful influence on all sentient beings. Then I visualized a white flame above the parasol reaching upward and stated, "I am the ether that moves the parasol of loving kindness and compassion." This flame represents infinite space or the void. I remembered that a few years back I had read in an old book where a few paragraphs talked about the stupas of India. Unfortunately, I cannot recall the name of the book. The author stated that an Indian elder took him aside and told him that the secret that activates the physical stupa are not just from the treasures held inside it or the prayers that went into building it, but that on top of the stupa, on the tip of the flame, is a small jewel or diamond. The jewel activates the entire stupa.

A few months back, in November 2016, I saw a vision of my angel kneeling with his hands held together in the prayer position, pointing up. This angel was fifty, if not a hundred, feet tall. Above his hands was a brilliant pure white diamond that rose to the heavens. I thus visualized that I was this angel with this pure radiant diamond standing at the very tip of the stupa. Its light reached to the heavens. After a few minutes, my crown chakra opened up. This is obviously a stupa through which transforming light enters. The diamond traveled from the tips of the angel's hands to the top of my head and my whole head became bright with light – the diamond mind.

On another date, my heart chakra opened when the diamond tip reached down through my body into my heart: The diamond heart. During the meditation, Tibetan tulkus raced, as though flying, into my heart chakra. I called out, "Divine ones come!" I wanted them to see what had happened. The Dalai Lama, the Karmapa, and Ammachi all came and walked about in the light of the diamond that reached up through to the heavens. Since then, the mind of clear light has been my companion in meditations. I often re-visualize the meditation process that I described above.

After performing this meditation about four times, another event happened. The diamond and stupa spontaneously transformed into a huge pillar connecting heaven and earth, like the cedar pole that runs through the center of the stupa. It is the spine of the meditator (posture is important while in meditation). The first time that the pillar was made in my visualization, there was a strong connection from Earth to heaven. The second time it was made the pure light came down from above through the pillar of my body and into the earth. I witnessed the light filling the planet underneath my feet. I heard the word "djet," the Ancient Egyptian symbol of power. A voice said to me clearly, "Remember that there are four of these."

Experience taught me that rising to the top to experience nirvana is not enough. That is not what it's about. Yes, there is an experience of bliss at the top, but the vision encourages the energy to flow down through all the chakras, to cleanse them. Once cleansed, the energy focuses on the heart chakra and nurtures first the person having the vision. Then the energy is sent out to the world causing transformative change (alchemy) and protection wherever it is needed. This is so important! It is a compassionate response to one's encounter with the Divine. It is a response of compassion to the world and those who live in it.

Once I meditated on the stupa and became it in my body, the harassing voices stopped. I was later told that this is because I had gone to a higher level and they no longer had access to me.

The Spirituality of the Stupa

The stupa is another form of alchemy. There are eight

different types of stupa, but they all transform energy. The stupa is an example of vertical spirituality that extends its energy horizontally. If you study its symbols and structure, you will learn why it is referred to as an image of the mind of Buddha. Ironically, as noted, it will take you to the djet of Ancient Egypt. The djet was the most powerful and most protective symbol in all of Ancient Egypt. This spirituality is still with us today!

Rising Above It

Since the experience with the stupa, I have learned that when something, someone, or an experience is bothersome to me it is wise to rise above it. There is a simple ritual that helps me. When confronted with negative or untruthful people or a negative situation, I ask that which is Divine and true to take me higher, beyond that which is false. First, I forgive everyone involved in the situation including myself. I then see myself rising above the situation, person, or false vision that I am experiencing and immediately I am taken above to a higher plane of existence and the suffering is no more. Sometimes I ask the Christ or the Lord Buddha to take me to a more loving experience beyond what I am experiencing. It works every time when I am sincere in my desire to be with and aligned with Buddha and Christ.

To go to the higher plane of existence I must be willing to let go of the trappings of the past and of the experience of suffering. Simply release it. This can be as simple as me not being around certain people or going to certain places anymore. Rising above a person or situation is often about changing our own personal habits. These difficult life situations always point to something greater. The question is, are we willing to go beyond time and space to get there. That is where our soul lives. It's just a different perspective.

Beyond Time and Space

When life on planet Earth is experienced as too much of a burden, we are often led to places beyond time and space. I recalled a time in 1978 when I was going through a lot of personal development struggles. I walked in nature regularly to help me get through it. While alone in the forest, I stopped often to sense and feel my surroundings. I stepped ever so slowly being conscious of every time I placed either foot to the earth. I did so with appreciation. It wasn't long, and though still walking, I awoke from a vision. Something took me to that timeless place of gratitude and joy. I saw a stepping up pyramid. Common people were at the bottom, one step up were the exemplary of the common people. Another step up revealed those genuinely striving to be closer to the Divine. A further step up were those on the spiritual path who had accomplished much. And, up again, were those spiritually close to the Divine in all they did. The next step revealed angels and holy men and women. This level was followed by the higher levels of powers and principalities along with archangels and finally, the Christ himself at the top with radiant light beaming from him in all directions. Equal love went out to all, no matter what level they were on. Each person on whatever level of the pyramid felt the depth of the experience of love based on their awareness and the service they provided. Hence, those at the bottom layer were not receiving less love but were receiving the fullness of Christ's love. They could only perceive His love as much as they sought to love and sought His presence. Such is true of all the levels.

This is one of several visions I've had that came from simply tuning in to nature.

But along with the visions of that time was the fact of a practice. I got up early every morning and meditated often alone in the chapel. I followed my breath and focused on Christ. As thoughts abounded, I simply returned to my breath and the image of Christ. I am reminded of a quote by His Holiness Ogyen Trinley Dorje, "We must strive for happiness by training our mind. If we manage to train our mind we can bring peace, happiness, harmony, and joy for all sentient beings" (Interview with H. H. the 17th Karmapa Ogyen Trinley Dorjee, by Tsering Dhondrup, The Times of Tibet, Feb, 2005).

Transformative Growth

Here's a simple, yet potent example of how transformative growth may happen in your life journey. While this scenario seems small, within it is a pattern that many people have revealed to me. The experience has left profound effects in those who reported. It is a pattern of revelation that people experience all the time at any level of the scenario described below. This particular scenario is placed with pet owners.

Intuition often begins with the realization that your pets are special to you.

That relationship then deepens to where you realize that your pet, horse, dog, cat, or whatever your pet, shows you that it has intelligence and understanding. Or, perhaps you one day realize that it loves you unconditionally. This moves you and you will never be the same. A relationship has begun.

The experience of intuition deepens when you realize that the animal is showing you things that it wants you to know. It is communicating with you. The animal is no longer a possession but a friend. It is relating to you personally about itself. It shows signs that it is taking care of you in return.

Eventually the relationship may deepen to where you begin to have an intuitive relationship with your pet. You are in your pet's presence and you are aware that your pet is communicating with you. This phenomenon happens because of the bond of love between you and your pet. Often it is the pet that loves you first. Eventually, it is possible to even receive an intuition about a need of your pet when you are not in the presence of your pet. Hence, the relationship continues to deepen.

But this is not the end, something even greater may happen. You are shown through your pet or another animal, any animal, that there is a connection between all beings. A mystery has opened up to you. You are aware of the great Oneness of all Being. The visible and invisible connection between yourself and all of nature begins revealing itself to you. What began with one animal is found in all of nature. You find yourself enwrapped with affection for nature. You begin to realize it is humans who seem to be the last creatures to get this. But you get it because of your fidelity to your pets and other animals as well as to all of nature.

Eventually, even more may open up to you if you are a sensitive trusted soul. Your pet, an animal, a tree, or some being of nature shows you something personal and relevant about yourself. It speaks to you. It speaks to your heart and you hear it. It is a miracle. A revelation. It changes your life. A creature gave you a personal revelation.

Beyond this, some animal or creature on this earth may give you protection or wisdom about creation that is profound. You connect to the fact that there is a life-

sibility for survival of the forest because they spread the fungi spores. Bear and many animals thrive on the salmon as well. The salmon start their lives in the forest streams and return to nurture the forest with nutrients from the ocean. The forest is a cacophony of intimacy, of harmony.

Compassion, A Quantum Leap

My mother once relayed a story about a woman who came from upstate New York to the small town of Humphrey, Nebraska. She said that no one knew this woman but that she rented a home just outside the city and became involved in the church. Now this was prior to the 1920's, an era before pharmaceutical medicines were developed. At church, there was a discussion about a woman who was dying. The family members had no one who could take care of her while she was in the dying process. In those days, there were few sedative medications. In the early 1900's and prior, it was common to tie people down in their bed and allow them to scream and writhe in pain. Death was messy, there were no such things as Pampers, or sanitary gloves.

The new arrival, however, offered to assist and even allowed the dying woman to be brought to her home on the edge of the city. This was seen as a very noble undertaking. Other women helped out.

When they observed this strong, patient woman in her middle thirties handle the patient, they realized that she was experienced with how to help very ill and actively dying people. She was often able to calm the dying person and had a routine that helped for cleaning and caring for the patient.

As time went on, this particular woman, with the help

bond between you and all of nature, and you question how you had never seen it before. You will never be the same. You yourself are now a creature of the Great Oneness. You communicate with all beings in heart and mind. You have become a bit of a mystic.

I know people who have had the same experiences with stones, feathers, and the Sacred Peace Pipe. Others have experienced it by being a stay-at-home mom or a spouse in a loving marriage. Over years the journey continues with slow but constant transformations. It all seems to happen through a relationship with pets or the stones, sacred objects, and other human beings. Yes, it happens in relationships with people too.

Biodiversity

There are so many different kinds of living things on this planet. Yet, they all seem to somehow work together, and science is proving that they do in fact work together. There is a harmony beyond what our eyes can see.

I just finished a video called "Magical Forests" in which Chris Packham explains the inextricably intertwined nature of nature. Salmon provide up to 70 or 80 percent of the growth in trees that live close by where salmon swim and spawn. This growth effect happens sometimes as far from the stream as 80 meters. The bears leave the salmon carcasses behind and the trees and all life benefits.

At the same time fungi form a network with trees and plants of large areas as wide as thirty and more meters. Fungi helps the plants to grow and even provide threads throughout the areas that trade off nutrients and even water. It is for the benefit of all the forest. Squirrels eat the fungi buds and thus spread the posof other women from the city, took in many people, one by one, to help them die. Her service to the community of Humphrey lasted twenty-five years. Then, finally, one day she herself became ill and quickly died.

My mother noted that the entire town and all the farmers from the surrounding area showed up for the funeral. It was a great tribute to a quiet compassionate stranger. Before she died and while she lay ill in bed, the neighbors asked her where she came from and how she had learned to do this amazing work. She said that she and her mother used to do this same work in a small town in New York State. However, when her mother died it was too much for her to live in that small city. So, she asked God where to go and she got the message loud and clear, "Go west." And she did go west until she found a home. Humphrey was the third small city that she attempted to stay in before she was accepted. It became her home.

This quiet woman's love and compassion deeply touched and transformed an entire town. This is power. This is alchemy.

Spiritual Alchemy

Spiritual alchemy is about having friends who dwell in high places. It begins with compassion, unconditional love, brotherhood, and harmony, any one of these. It can also begin with something like truth, or peace. At first one becomes compassionate by intention of the heart and then performing compassionate deeds. If one has zeal, he or she eventually embodies compassion. It is a realization that we are not alone and the suffering of one affects all others. Then compassion becomes the portal. Literally compassion, love, brotherhood, etc., are the portals to the new perceptions of the new age into which we are now seated. But we are not alone. The above virtues will draw benevolent beings to your side; spirits, angels, archangels, and great master teachers will come to your aid.

Transformation and Meditation

In my morning meditation, I often visualize light shining through my chakras and body. Sometimes I visualize three blue globes, one at my brow just above my nose and one in each hand, which are on my lap. I then imagine a blue line connecting the three globes forming a triangle. While holding this visual I asked for humility, correct thoughts, correct emotion, and correct attitudes for the service of my true calling. Sometimes I also call upon the brotherhood or angels of the blue light ray.

This visualization opens parts of me to other dimensions. I have learned that meditation with colors reshapes my present, hence, allowing the future. I believe that meditation with colors dispels blockages and negative forces causing a realignment for what is to come for my higher purpose and calling. Before I begin a meditation with color, I ask the higher guides that everything in my charge comes to its correct order and keeping for my true authentic calling and service. Generally, I experience that something happens. At times, I feel that something is removed, or, that something opens up for me. I often feel reassured during or after such an exercise.

I do not do these things alone. I call upon the angels, the Christ, the masters, and the brotherhood of the blue light ray. These beings are willing to help me. They orchestrate my life and realign it with all that is around me on this Earth plane for my highest good. Meditation and prayers with the masters and guides produce the necessary personal alchemical change to help fulfill our purpose. As we change, we are able to help transform the world about us.

About That Color Blue

The study of the physics of color light rays reveals that certain color waves do not have as much force as other colors. The ultraviolet light color blue has a much higher vibration than red, yellow, or orange. Though these rays travel in a straight line they are also light waves. However, unlike the color red, the blue wave pattern is not spread out as far. Therefore, the color blue has more force in its influence on other objects upon impact. With the force of the blue light ray, electrons move out of the way and therefore cause a reshaping of atoms and molecules. This happens much more from the force of a blue ray than a red color ray. It is a matter of power.

From a metaphysical perspective, meditation with the colors blue, indigo, and purple appear to cause creative projects to happen at a faster rate and with more force and power than if meditating with the color red, yellow or orange. This is not to say that the three colors mentioned should not be used for meditation. They are very good colors for grounding and creativity. They are also protective colors. Meditation and visualization with colors provides opportunity for transformation especially when used with intention.

The base chakra is associated with the color red, the second is orange, the third yellow, on through the colors of the rainbow. If a person operates mainly through the lower chakras, he or she has less power than persons who vibrate from not only the lower but also the upper chakras. Yet, even if a person operates out of all of the chakras but the lower chakras are not open and whole it is difficult to advance. All the chakras should be encouraged to be open and whole. People who have not developed their upper chakras cannot harm you if all of your vibration centers are healthy and functioning well. That is why people call upon the master's when they feel to be in any kind of danger. The spiritual energy of Buddha, Christ or Krishna, etc., are much higher than the energies of the material plane. These beings, by their mere presence, transform energies. All one need do is call upon them and ask for their presence. I call upon Christ daily with profound results and have called upon Avalokiteshvara's name as a mantra while visualizing his presence. I watched and felt transformation happen immediately. Calling upon the masters, Buddhas, and archangels is potent spiritual alchemy, and results are often immediate.

Love Is Alchemy

When you call upon these higher beings and desire their full presence with you, evil diminishes. That is how exorcisms are performed. One does not fight evil! One brings higher powers in! It is that simple, and it is very effective. Sometimes all that is required of us is to step up the spiritual ladder one or two rungs. Further, one should not tread into a situation where evil is said or known to be present. This may be stepping down and into someone else's level of existence. Walk away from it and do prayers from a safe place of love and light (if it's your business to do so). Even then, some people and situations are very dark, and I do not confront them even from a distance. I ask the angels and masters to take care of the situation for me. I do this by visualizing the protector Archangel Michael or the Master Jesus, but first ask protection for myself. Then I ask them to send love and light to the person or situation involved. Allow all cords of destruction to be cut and do not think about that person or situation from a troubled point of view. To walk into or think yourself into an evil or dark situation often leads one to be caught in its web.

One must measure the severity of negative forces before taking them on. There is much happening in the world that I pray about, but it is not always my place to confront what is happening. If you are in a difficult or negative situation, however, you do well to not ignore it but act immediately. Results happen best if one is a regular meditator and has a loving relationship with the Divine. Relationship connotes presence, does it not? Presence emanates a vibration. If the vibration is strong, negativity leaves. Love is the highest form of spiritual presence.

I was once informed by a medicine man that when two people love each other deeply and maintain that love between themselves and in their family, no witchcraft or sorcery could touch them. Love is the ultimate, most powerful virtue. It is the power of Christ. It is the force of St Michael. Forgive your enemies, and they have no attachment to you. If you forgive someone, there is an immediate alchemical transformation. This is because your body and psyche are set free of that burden.

Have you thought of forgiving your CEOs, politicians, and world leaders, etc.? They have much less effect on you if you forgive them regularly. As long as you are entrapped by your anger toward someone (anyone), you cannot see through what these people are doing. When you see through what people are doing, they and their actions affect you much less. When they do something that disturbs you again you forgive again but use the anger created by the injustice to create an appropriate rebuttal or action. Forgiveness is an act of love for yourself and others. Love helps us to be aware of what is going on in our personal lives and the world. This is because love is free of negative attachments.

If you find yourself surrounded by people who just do not care about you or others, you need to ask Spirit immediately where you belong because you do not belong there. Don't think you can change them or take them down. Get out of there!

A Powerful Forgiveness Exercise

Have you ever tried sending yourself love while looking into a mirror? This is a powerful exercise. Begin by calling upon your spiritual guides and the great spiritual master or teacher you rely on. Then spend about two to five minutes looking into a mirror saying to yourself with heartfelt energy, "I love you." You will accomplish much. But follow this with two to five minutes saying, "I love you and I forgive you." You may want to continue the meditation by telling yourself (while looking into the mirror) that you love yourself unconditionally and forgive yourself in this and all of your life-times. This is a powerful exercise that reaps great benefit when repeated for twenty-one days.

I highly suggest you follow this exercise by again looking into the mirror. This time imagine yourself speaking to each of your immediate family members and possibly some of your friends or acquaintances. Say with love and meaning, "I love you and, I forgive you." After a few minutes of this exercise, you can say, "I love you and I forgive you in this lifetime and in all other lifetimes that we have ever known each other." If the words are said with love and genuine sincerity, these exercises are powerful and will launch you forward on your spiritual journey. We are held back by many attachments due to unresolved or unforgiving anger. Anger is a toxic poison.

But forgiving is not enough. We have to reflect about our part in the situation that occurred. For some people un-forgiveness has to do with anger. For others, it has to do with stubbornness. Sometimes we do well to look at what really happened between ourselves and another person with new eyes. Perhaps from the eyes of the other person involved. Was it a matter of money? Then what drives your attachment to money, and what drives the other persons attachment to money? If un-forgiveness is about relationship, then where does unconditional or detached love fit into the picture? There are many lenses through which we need to study what forgiveness and un-forgiveness are all about. We cannot do this if we are attached to the situation. This means letting go of judgments if possible and trying to see the situation with the eyes of compassion. Compassion requires a new blueprint for looking at a situation. This means we have to let go of the old habit of how we have looked at other people or situations. Through practice, compassion becomes our new road map.

The Peacock and the Roadrunner

What is so powerful about the beautiful peacock and its cousin, the small roadrunner, is that they eat poisonous snakes. The poison is transmuted and transformed into nourishment in their bodies. This is alchemy.

Likewise, when we truly forgive someone the poison is consumed by love and compassion for oneself and the other. A tremendous transformation occurs. When we forgive someone personal growth usually follows. This is because the part of our selves that wanted to hold on to not forgiving shows its face and has to be dealt with. The universal law is that we are all intimately connected and in our authentic selves all of us are meant to live in harmony. This is why the virtues of love and compassion draw us closer to enlightenment.

Alchemy is all About Transformation, Change, and Growth

There are many people who perform meditation without a spiritual connection. They want the benefits of meditation but without spiritual ascension. Often there are people whose aim and goal in meditation is for financial success and material comforts. But, if they are not developed in their upper chakras, they remain on the same level of vibration as greed and envy and have little protection unless they are very experienced and really know themselves.

Most spiritual battles take place within us. This is because spiritual battles require a choice. Just as forgiveness is a choice, all the habits that we have are choices about how we want to live and be in the world. All choices we make are decisions about how we are going to live in this world. From a spiritual perspective, a successful choice requires a higher or at least a better value, a higher vibration, a better or higher wisdom or knowledge. Part of the purpose of struggle on this planet is to help us make better choices for ourselves. When we elevate ourselves spiritually, we will automatically be in the midst of change. Yet most of us fight change. Given our present planetary situation, change from within is the only safe road. If spiritual forces direct the changes you are making from within, then changes from without will support you. The soul is the guardian of transformation.

Buddhists try to embrace change as a means of growth, superseding the old and embracing the new wisdom. Nothing is permanent. Dedication to the teachings of the Buddha and the higher spiritual laws is the path to enlightenment. Many of these same laws are found in sacred scriptures and sutras from the world religions. The Christian Bible is full of such wisdom, the law of love being the highest law.

In the Gospels Jesus speaks most about the kingdom of God, then about forgiveness, then about having a relationship to the Father, and then about love (in that order). Many scripture theologians argue that it is highly doubtful that Jesus was concerned about establishing a church at all. Rather he was about awakening us to the kingdom of God, which is within. Of the numerous world religions I have studied, the Hindu religion probably most represents and adheres to the value that the kingdom of God that is within. To come to know the God within allows it to be expressed in the world as a Christ being, and enlightened being. That is what a Sadhu is meant to be. This means that there has been a total transformation of the psyche and body to reflect Divinity. Hence, with an enlightened being, the soul expresses itself completely and freely.

Alchemy and the Body

I have studied alchemy only to come to the conclusion that alchemy is nothing more than the path to enlightenment. We are spiritual beings in a body. Therefore, we will do well to balance above and below.

The polarities of the mind and body need to be balanced (thought and emotion, male and female, etc.) while we make this ascension. In other words, we need to live in harmony within our own mind, in our own body, and with all beings while we ascend toward enlightenment. That is the crux of alchemy. While we ascend, we do not leave the earth and its inhabitants behind but rather we affect all beings and even the material planet. All is a reflection of the Divine and it is all returning to Divinity. Sometimes the best way for things to return to the Divine is for them to dissolve.

This is why keeping harmony within the mind demands discipline. If the mind is not disciplined through exercises like meditation and writing, it will be difficult to hone the mind to be of service for our benefit. All spiritualities also discipline the body as part of spiritual growth.

Seeds of Wisdom

The practitioners of the world religions have learned that some traditions, practices, and their associating beliefs have worked well and consistently over millennia. Those beliefs and practices are not many in number, nor have they changed over the centuries. Many religious traditions, practices, and beliefs connect us to the higher laws and practices that are in place beyond the earth plane. One could write an entire thesis on the Christian mass and what in it has changed over the years, and what in it has been retained as the core beliefs that sustain Christianity. One needs to take note that most of the Christian mass rituals (as with other Christian rituals) have been borrowed from other traditions over time. The original core meanings of these rituals point to the power of the Divine and give direction toward what sustains us and what we need to become. What sustains us has little to do with material comforts. The inner core meaning, the seeds of wisdom are available to us regularly on a daily basis if we are attentive.

    I have come to learn that it is often the small realizations that sustain me. More often than not, it is the little things that connect me to the greater core meaning of life. These come as intuitions and Ah-Ha moments. One day, I walked away from the writing table and ever so naturally my mind continued to ramble. This happens when I perform household tasks, and personal care stuff that just needs to be done now and then. While washing and drying dishes, mopping or vacuuming the floor, doing laundry, or cutting potatoes, the mind wanders. But having been at my writing table and having meditated just before that, the underlying thoughts about the topic of my writing crept to surface from the unconscious. Hence, the rambling mind immediately began picking up on a flow of thoughts and ideas. These inspirational ramblings happen. It is a continuation of the meditation performed prior, and the discipline of writing. This of course, happens best if meditation and writing are regular daily habits. It is in the rambling that the unconscious or the super conscious speaks to us. One must learn to be conscious of the rambling. Meditation and other spiritual practices slow the emotional and worry aspects of the mind down and hence open the way for the flow of wisdom.

    By the same principle, we are informed through the consciousness level we operate out of. To the degree that we have allowed ourselves to rise in spiritual awareness or consciousness is the degree to which we are inspired in the mind's rambling moments. This rambling is the mind reflecting. It is like a state of daydreaming, but really, we are pondering. When we are able to catch (or be in) the moment in which the rambling takes place we can receive inspiration. Meditation is key because through the practice of a daily discipline it is the higher mind that reflects through us. When the higher mind reflects through us transformation occurs. This is alchemy.

How Alchemy Unfolds in my Daily Life and Prayer

One morning my body energy was feeling quite low. I didn't know how I was going to complete the tasks of the day. I began by treating myself to a hot cup of yerba matta tea, which is known to raise one's level of relaxed awareness. After meditation and prayers, I felt to go to back to bed to rest for a while. I awoke from a meditative state and realized I was in conversation with someone. He told me that another person will be in charge of my duties at this time and encouraged me to rest. Feeling my tiredness, I held my thumbs for a few minutes then my ring fingers, then my forefingers, then my middle fingers. While holding each middle finger, I called upon the archangel Zadkiel (the angel of mercy) and asked that any anger in my body be turned to peace and mercy within me. I then proceeded to send purple light through my chakras for a few minutes and went into a trance. The person or being who had been speaking to me earlier came to me again. He said that what I was doing, meaning holding my fingers and sending out purple light with the assistance of the angels, is very powerful. After a few minutes I got up and felt a complete shift had taken place in my energy field. I was in a very relaxed state of being which allowed for higher awareness.

This was a moment of awareness that allowed me to catch up on much needed energy. I ended up doing many small tasks that day that needed attention. Each moment is dependent upon another moment. I would not have experienced the moment of much needed rest and rejuvenation had I not listened to the voice. I would not have heard the voice had I not meditated regularly as a practice. I would not have known to intuitively hold my fingers had I not taken a class about Jin Shin Jyutsu. That one moment was an accumulation of moments and decisions of the past all come into one. It was a small moment of enlightened consciousness that I acted upon. By the end of my day many small tasks that were waiting to be completed were completed and I was feeling caught up, rested, and peaceful.

We all have moments of enlightened consciousness. But consciousness is not something that can be had or possessed. A material thing can be bought, but consciousness is not like a material thing. Consciousness is within, it is everywhere, is not a possession, but never leaves you. It exists within a continuous presence potential that can be born within our every word and action. It flows from living life.

The Master Visits

At 5:30 a.m., on January 19, 2016, I saw a holy man whom I presume was the Master Jesus. He came through from another dimension, stood in front of me and said, "Gary, if you give me your heart, I will give you mine." He then returned to the other dimension, as quickly as he had arrived. His presence left me in a state of awe and wonder. He was of pure beautiful light. If we regularly welcome the master, the master will visit.

During meditation, I regularly visualize and call upon the Light of Christ. I visualize the Light coming through me and filling me, expanding me with faith, hope, love, and health. I request for and see myself in a field of protection. I often ask the Christ to dwell in my heart area. Then I visualize that this light is expanding through my person and being, and I allow myself to feel what that light is doing to me. At times, I visualize and call upon the Mother Mary and do the same with her image and light. This brings me to the protection and love that comes from the feminine. We may call upon them and imagine their energy of light expand throughout and around our bodies. This exercise energizes my day. It puts order into the world within and around me. Sometimes there is an automatic response and that light goes all by itself through my body to someone in need. This automatic response shows me that at some level I am in harmony with other beings. I therefore often say the mantra, "I am One with God," or "God and I are One."

I believe that the energy and life and light of the Great Ones is teleported, or brought into, and through anyone who desires to participate with the Light and allow it. I believe that love, and intention (or willpower) are two of the great powers of the universe. A third power is encapsulated in the words "believe" or "faith." You cannot have willpower unless belief is contained within it. Will is belief and intention. If you apply belief, and intention with love you have energy or force (the power of the three virtues working in harmony), or, one could say that you have creative energy. What is intended through love becomes. What are your intentions? If your intentions are united with the intentions of the Divine, amazing things will happen. If your intentions are wrapped up in survival (which is fear based), materialism, fame, or other non-virtuous thoughts, you will be slow to experience the grace of God.

What if, there is a plan for you while you are here on this earth? Then it follows that you might want to know what that plan is. It follows that you will want to conform to following or becoming the plan of God in your life by applying intention and love in a way that is in harmony with the Divine. If you desire it and work for it, you will become it, because its seeds are already within you. I believe that the Divine plan that is seeded within us is a quantum leap waiting to happen.

Could it be that the plan inherited for this lifetime, if there is a plan and there are consecutive lifetimes, comes from that which has been built from previous existences? Perhaps this is so because in the theory of relativity, time and space are one? Hence if one experiences beyond time, beyond thought and form, does one not receive or experience from a source beyond that which is consciously known. This is the realm of Super-Consciousness, the Christ Mind, the Buddha mind.

The Theory of Relativity

The Theory of Relativity suggests that time slows down to accommodate movement. But it is said; because we cannot go fast enough to equal or exceed the speed of light, we cannot reverse time. This I believe is false because we are made of light, and when we are in a high state of meditation it is possible to experience that time and space disappear. Speed is measured by time. If time and space disappear, then that means at times when space and time seem to have disappeared, we have gone beyond the speed of light, as it is scientifically known in this dimension. That is why those who practice meditation often experience a healing of the past. It is because in meditation they go beyond time and space, beyond this dimension. Perhaps a transformation of the past is possible because we have gone to the Source from which light comes in the first place. All existing things are made of light, or, in the case of the void space, of the absence of visible light.

Light as we know it is composed of mass/energy/speed or movement ($E=mc^2$). This means that time and space are involved in the essence of the equation for light. Yet, the trained meditator experiences themselves beyond time and space. Is this because one has gone beyond the speed of light, to a light source that does not have time involved in its equation? What if, in such a place (if it is a place at all), one may re-experience, or remake the past and it becomes healed? It was merely a creation erased and perhaps recreated. If a meditator begins with an intention, a thought of forgiveness, or an imagined recreation of what happened in the past, and then goes into that timeless state, is the present therefore changed because how one has perceived the past has changed? I have experienced changes of this sort and believe it is real. The past can be recreated and healed.

Buddhists refer to the Mind of Clear Light, which is perceptible through consciousness, yet it is an invisible Light that is the Source from which all things are made. It is made of only positive virtues such as love, compassion, wisdom, etc. Therefore, exposing oneself to the wounds of the past while in the state of the Mind of Clear Light may cause a change in perspective, a total healing of what was. The new perspective becomes conscious when one comes out of the meditation, and because of the intention to forgive, the wound is no more. The present is not what it was just moments before. One is free and unbound from the past. Creative new potential is at one's disposal.

One way that consciousness moves forward is relative to the human ability to forgive and be compassionate. Forgiveness is an act of simultaneous compassion toward oneself and others. This I shall call the consciousness of becoming. With the consciousness of becoming we transcend time and space and Light serves us because we are made of Light. Therefore, in our natural human state we are transformers and have the ability to forgive and be compassionate. Healing and consciousness are in proportion to a person's active participation with and use of the light of which he/she is made. We can consciously create a new reality, or at least recreate our perception of reality as we have known it.

That being said, I propose that some types of meditation can be all about light and becoming. The more humanity uses light in this fashion, the quicker the advancement of science and humanity. Humanity and science are not separate. Therefore, humanity and scientific advancement are not separate. Experience is relative to events experienced. This is the new theory of science. Yet, you are not your experiences but merely experiencing.

At the same time, from another perspective, you are not your thoughts. You are not your emotions. You are not even your daily habits unless you have identified with them. While you are not your experiences, even so, it is through our experiences that we place an identity on to others and ourselves. In essence, that is not who we are. Who then are you in essence?

The essence of you is that part of you that entered the physical world that is you authentically. It is not dependent on anything for its creation. In essence you are Light, a part of the Divine Essence. In essence, you are beyond thought and form, and beyond duality. You are a harmonious being.

Seeds to Ponder

A seed contains the essence and potential of the whole plant. Who then are we, and what is our potential? Human beings live and grow through experience, and the knowledge that comes through life always leads us to something beyond, or deeper within. Because we experience, we are in a constant state of becoming. When we finish with an experience, have processed it and released it we go on to other experiences. Hence, we are not our experiences, but something more. Rather, we are the essence of the Pure Light from which we have come. We are the essence of the Source itself. We do not experience that we are "That" because we have an ego that demands to experience power, or a unique personality. The ego wants to have an identity. But in essence, it has none. Through experience, especially during meditation, being present, through the practice of the virtues, or through yoga, we are taken to something of greater depth, of greater meaning, of a furthering of consciousness. The ego has no grip there, no identity. This is because the virtues are by nature transformative, hence, alchemical.

Relativity always works in harmony with the law, but it accommodates the viewer through whom it is experienced. Without this harmony we could not survive. The confinement of time accommodates the viewer along with the experience of physicality and space. Without what we call the Theory of Relativity all would be chaos or disharmony. We experience that we influence the world about us. A sense of order is given to relative events so that our limited mentality feels secure. Who are you, that you should be so accommodated? Well, you are the experience of the One, great Essence, or Source from which we all come. That there is an order to the universe is true. Otherwise scientific theory would not work. And, neither Tibetan and other Buddhist traditions nor the Buddha himself would be able to come up with relevant truths that have worked over millennia of time. When a person is in deep meditation she or he is in harmony with all beings. This means that somehow relativity and meditation go hand in hand. Yet, beyond meditation, in everyday life we remain deeply interconnected to all that is because we are made of the same Source, Clear Light.

Meditation is very accommodating to the experience of the Theory of Relativity. Through meditation, we gain contact with the soul, which is in tune with the harmony of relativity. The soul, which is beyond time and place, balances our lives. It is greater and wiser than we are. Yet, it humbly serves us. We sit back and observe, or experience, as it brings us to harmony. It brings order to chaos. Relativity happens best and more often through participation in a practice that gets us in contact with the soul. It even has the power to heal wounded or broken hearts. What a great and beautiful science to participate in.

In regard to the Theory of Relativity, we are not faced with the question of whether God or Spirit or powers exist or do not exist. Rather, it is a question of having a science that participates with the powers that be, even when they appear to be chaotic. Relativity is a science that is intimately experienced, the numinous and humanity are, in reality, One. It is as simple as coming to your breath. Attentive presence to breath gives experience to Oneness with all beings; even the Universe.

There ought be no surprise then that Bodhisattvas and Enlightened beings are compassionate to all beings. Enlightened ones return again and again to the timeless circle of life to be compassionate, to bring an end to suffering. They are in harmony with the pulse of the Universe, where All is Harmony, All is One, in the same way Jesus Christ was resurrected taking him beyond the limitations of the physical body and temporal existence. This frees him to continuously serve humanity and all created things without limitation. The Buddha and the Christ are united with the essence of Source, yet remain to teach, care for, and aid those who seek transformation. They remain in the state of transformation for the sake of all other beings. This is alchemy.

Chapter 4
The Soul and Abundance

What Does Having Abundance Mean for You?

Do you feel trapped at your workplace? Do you feel that the company or corporation you work for is now leaning toward the slavery of its employees? Are you in a position at your job where your gifts and talents are able to shine forth? Are you able to climb the ladder to success at your current job? Many people are asking these questions with dissatisfaction. Many are faced with getting out of the rut by a change of attitude, a change within yourself, or possibly a change of job.

If you are dissatisfied with your current job you would do well to ask yourself, what does the soul want me to do? If you dislike your job, it affects your entire person – mentally, emotionally, physically, and spiritually. Your connection with your soul is your abundance. This is so because the soul reveals to you your calling. The soul is the connection that makes all other connections work in your behalf, for what you really need. The soul is interested in all of your needs and concerns. In fact, the soul governs what abundance is for you. Here is a list of questions to ponder:

What is abundance for you? Is it being a mother or father?

Is it being a poet, a painter, or writer?

Is it having very good friends?

Is abundance about being the best that you can be?

Is abundance about being happy, whatever happy is for you?

Is abundance for you about being in nature with your

horses and dogs?

Is abundance about feeling secure?

Is abundance for you about having a rewarding spiritual life?

Is abundance about having a healthy, wholesome, and beautiful body?

Is abundance about being a member of a wonderful family, and having the best spouse ever?

Or do you perceive that abundance is just and only about having a job that brings in money?

This chapter argues that abundance arises from the soul and knowing and being what the soul wants for you is your abundance. Abundance does require the use of your gifts and talents. You are unique, and your needs and experiences are unique. At the center of you is a desired fulfillment. Getting to know what is at the center of you is your abundance. The gifts that you manifest are leading up to, or, are fulfilling the desired fulfillment of your soul. That desire may change over time as you change and experience life. The soul as the connector to harmony knows your deepest need as seen from the eyes of Divinity. There may be many steps required to get to your deepest need, but the soul will help you accomplish all of them as you climb the ladder of fulfillment.

The Realization of Abundance

I was not faced with the need to have an abundant life until I acquired a lot of debt. Up to that point I had always been provided for and probably didn't even give it a thought that there is something called abundance that watches over me. How does one call it? Perhaps it is the nature of the universe itself, who, like a mother, looks after her own. Is there an angel of abundance? Or, is it perhaps an inheritance, something that belongs to me by right of birth? Ironically through acquiring debt I have become aware of the abundance that is forever with me. Though I have been through some very difficult times I have always been cared for. All of my needs have been met. The awareness that my needs are being met allows me to move forward to a successful future. However, if I did not take action regarding my debt, I would live in stagnation, worry, and fear. Life demands participation.

I actively participated in the building of a financial plan so that I could move forward into the future. This project became an opportunity for me to be a co-creator with the universe in its care for me. When I made my first payment to the government toward my student loan debt, joy ran through my body. I remember the feeling in the face of what seemed an impossible task. With a few lifestyle adjustments, I'm doing it. It's working for me. I am provided for.

So how is this different from any other situation or problem we have on planet earth? It's not. We humans are co-creators of our earthly existence. We must move beyond worry and fear to investigate the facts. We have to get personally involved in our life situation and search for a plan. This is our planet. To the degree that we work with the Universal Forces of Good for the good of all, is to the degree that They will bless us.

What is Abundance?

Do you limit your abundance? Another way of looking at abundance is to say that abundance is whatever your greatest desire is. It may be a desire that you were born with. If you believe that your greatest desire is to have material things or money, then that is what abundance is for you. If you believe that your greatest desire is peace, or to wage war, or if you believe it is to have a relationship, or just having a sex partner, then, that is what abundance is for you. And those things may very well be what you will get in return for the energy that you put into your desire. This means that we have to know from deep within what the soul's desire is for us.

For many people, a happy family is all they want. That is their abundance. For the dedicated Buddhist, abundance is an end to suffering for all beings. They choose a higher value. For the Master Jesus, abundance meant to be One with the Father. Is that what the average Christian desires as their first and most important desire?

If it is true that abundance expresses as your greatest desire then, it is good to ask, "What is my deepest desire, my deepest longing, hope, or dream?" That is the abundance you are actually seeking. But is it truly in harmony with what the soul is seeking? What is the souls desire for you?

I personally believe that most people do not ever learn what the great desire of the soul is for them. Many of us make changes throughout our lives but never reach that full potential or perhaps are aware of it but do not know how to become it. Others simply choose to not go there. Until we find the desire of the soul, we experience an inner longing. There is a feeling that there has to be something more. One feels unfulfilled or out of place.

The Saboteur

We learn how to acquire the soul's passion step by step. Our needs in the world matter to the soul. A person may desire a nice apartment in a particular area of town. But if he is spending his available money on material objects, extravagant vacations, or late evenings at the bar, it may be difficult to gain the hoped-for dream. Clearly the finances needed to fulfill the dream are being given to the individual. But if a person is spending what is available on extra or unnecessary things then the spiritual world cannot help that individual fulfill his or her desire.

The dreamer does well to question what part of himself or herself sabotages the valued goal. Self-sabotage runs amok among human beings. For many people it is the crux of the "problem" of unmet needs, desires, and goals. Abundance remains an unfulfilled dream waiting in the distance. Many people affirm what they want on a daily basis through affirmations. But those who accomplish their goals realize that it is important to change habits that directly counter receiving their goal. Learning what those habits are is of equal importance. One cannot work toward a goal while at the same time unconsciously operating counter to it. Yet, that is a common phenomenon.

If you want to learn what self-sabotage is all about, I suggest you have a chat with a couple of guys and gals who have attained sobriety and belong to an Alcoholics Anonymous group. Ask them to tell you their story. These people understand what self-sabotage is at a core level because they cannot afford to make a mistake. Through trial and error, they have learned how to deal with the inner saboteur. Otherwise they could not remain healthy members of our society. Dealing with unhealthy habits is what leads to success. We all learn by trial and error in both the material and spiritual worlds. But AA members rely on more than processing their lives and honesty to fulfill their hopes and dreams. They believe in a Higher Power.

The Higher Power

This leads us to important questions. What does the Higher Power, or God, see as abundance for you? Are you aligned with the calling that the Divine has for you (The soul's desire)?

If you ask these questions and align yourself with the desired goal of your true calling, then the abundance you seek is in alignment with the Divine. Then, your desired abundance will be in alignment with your authentic gifts and talents. If you are aligned with your life's calling, then how can you be denied of your goal if you are proceeding to work toward it? The Divine, however, does not promise wealth but provides our needs if we are in tune with our calling. What is so ironic about following Divine guidance is that one never knows the outcome or the timing of when or how something is going to happen. This requires faith in the process and in Divine timing.

Aligning Yourself with Your True Calling

The only way to align yourself with your authentic calling is to have a relationship with the Divine. Seek your calling, through prayer, daily meditation etc. It helps to write a note with a single question to Spirit and place it beside your bed table. If you get a dream write it down immediately. The answers will come in your dreams.

Aside from the goal to have a livelihood that I enjoy, wherein I express my authentic gifts and talents as seen from the eyes of Spirit, I have the goal to live safely and comfortably, to have all my needs met. I'd like to have enough to not need to worry and to be able to be generous so I can help others. These are simple but important goals.

Consciousness and Abundance

There is nothing wrong with having possessions or being wealthy. All that matters regarding the laws of the universe is how one appreciates and uses wealth. If it is used as a means to enjoy life, there is nothing wrong with that. If it is used for fame or to look down on others, to compare, or live in a competitive state, then the laws of the universe will not support you. Likewise, if one is wealthy but greedy to have more something is wrong. Greed never serves. If you have wealth in abundance and your neighbors are hungry but you have not shared, you are not in harmony with the spiritual law of universal brotherhood. Recently, the Tibetan Buddhist Karmapa stated that it is best for us to think that in actuality we all know each other: That before we incarnated every person on this planet harmoniously agreed to live on planet Earth to support each other, the Earth, and all other life (paraphrased). This is the Law of Brotherhood. We are born to be compassionate and kind. In many cases this means sharing our resources.

Being that the earth is made of energy, and in harmony with quantum physics, if all is energy then there are higher values than material things. Naturally, the poor who are in need of a home more than likely value food or a home as their most important need of the time. But what is your greatest hoped for goal? The goals for the Buddha, Islamic mystics, Hindu and Christian saints are to obtain and live by higher values.

When looking at abundance it is best to think both physically and spiritually. By spiritually, I mean to think of values that you truly desire for yourself and others.

For instance, I know a number of young men and women who are looking to get married. If they come to me seriously questioning how to go about looking for a partner, I have questions for them. Do you want a marriage because it is the expected thing to do? Do you want a marriage that looks good to yourself and others because of wealth, family name, etc.? Rather, you might want a marriage that is built on love and commitment, an authentic relationship. Need I remind the reader that all relationships involve work and sacrifice? Just as successful relationships require a lot of us, so does a life of abundance. Hopefully your relationship is part of your abundance. Mine is! But our relationship is at times hard work for both of us. Yet our commitment to each other has paid off many times. This is abundance! This is a blessing! It is not possible to have a sustaining blessed union without practicing the virtues. Hence, being that love is the most important of all the virtues, when focusing on the relationship, I believe that love is the answer.

There was a period of time when I was a massage therapist. A gentleman from the Marina in San Francisco arrived for a massage. He made it clear to me that he had money and I was good looking. He asked me right then and there if I would marry him because he would look good in public when we went out together. He informed me that I could continue my massage therapy business and would never have to worry about anything else. This would have been a materialistic marriage. I knew immediately that to marry him would have been a very lonely experience for me. He was a very nice guy but did not have a spiritual bone in his body. Nor, obviously, did he have relationship skills. I would have starved spiritually in this relationship. It would have been a disaster for me.

There is a great danger if one is looking to be cared for in a relationship. There is also a danger in looking to care for someone else. A marriage is built on love. When I was in theology training for the priesthood, it was made clear to students by our instructors that a priest or minister does not marry a couple. Rather he or she witnesses the marriage. In the Christian churches it is God or Christ who marries a couple to each other. God is love. That is sacred ground. What God has joined let no one divide. Marriage has little to do with material wealth. Abundance is finding your true-life partner, someone that you deeply love. If you decide to marry the one you love, then your marriage is a commitment to your abundance. This is soulful living.

For many people, material things are important, for others material things are not so important. Hospice patients often tell me that as they approach the end of their life, what they most value for their children is that they get along with one another. For them, it is the single most desired value in their consciousness. Some of them obtain it and some do not. All people have a free will, so if the children do not have the same value as their parents and grandparents the outcome will be different from the desires of their parents.

I recently met a woman on hospice who was in her nineties. She said that due to her illness she had spent her entire savings of $850,000. She said that she would have liked it more if her children received that money but noted that she is satisfied because her children like each other and get along. Peace between her children was her most important value and acknowledging that, she died in peace. That is abundance.

Because our world is entwined with a world of other

people it is good to look at the material things we want to have and ask if values are involved. Bob Proctor, Mary Morrissey, and Napoleon Hill have stated, "It's not about the money." Money is energy. But the spiritual values of compassion, harmony, kindness, truth, and love are sources of tremendous energy. When we practice the virtues, we are affirming universal values that are in alignment with universal laws? The universal spiritual laws oversee everything that exists. Therefore, if you live in harmony with the virtues, the universal laws behind them will support you. Devotion to the Divine is also a protective, resourceful virtue, that brings prosperity. A successful spiritual life demands work on both the spiritual and temporal planes.

What you most desire, or how much you put into making your desire a reality affects your future. You have the power to influence not only your own future, but you have the ability to influence the whole earth and beyond. But to do so one has to have an intention and use the imagination. Intention and imagination are so very important. They are the tools of the creative or inventive personality. We use intention and imagination to flesh out a world of being. All people use them. As stated above, whatever your hopes, your aspirations, desires, yearnings, longings, these are your intended affirmations. The creative process is constantly active within us. We are by nature creative beings. Our thoughts, decisions, actions, and words continuously affect the world around us.

Another irony as stated above, though we create continuously we also destroy our creations and aspirations continuously through our thoughts, beliefs and habits. The average person does not realize that restraining personal beliefs and belief systems are what we use to either destroy or build our new ideas and lives.

What if you believe that you are not worthy to be wealthy? I was taught that. I was also taught that life is supposed to be hard and hard work to the end. That's what my parents did. When I signed up for an art class in college, my parents forbade it as a waste of time. I was paying for my own education but obeyed them and signed out of the class immediately. Yet, it was a class that I really wanted to take. But it was my belief that I was never supposed to disappoint my parents. Unfortunately, I adopted for myself the belief that artwork and creativity were a waste of time. I was also taught that artists suffered lives of poverty.

What lies do you tell yourself, or your family and friends? According to my horoscope chart I am an intensely creative person. Much of what was meant for me to enjoy was destroyed or given over to false assumptions and beliefs. Through our beliefs and words we either create or destroy ours and others abundance. We limit the activity of the soul through our choice of words.

In his book *Outwitting the Devil*, Napoleon Hill states that most habits and beliefs we live by are adopted and that many beliefs of the past affirmed that we were born evil, bad, or with a blemish on our soul. These beliefs affect us on deep levels. The voice of the soul is shut out or off. Then we cannot hear the soul's advice for us, we work against it because of belief systems. But when ignited, the soul is an incredibly powerful thing, connecting us to all other beings and heeding us to attend to that which is Divine.

Bob Proctor turns soul-destroying lies around in the title of his book, "You Were Born Rich." Said another way, "you were born an abundant being." We are born as children of a Pure Divine Source. Some Hindu's say that we were born with the memory of the Life-Source inherent in us. Hence, the spark of the Divine is within us. We are authentic children of the Source of all creation! Do you believe that? What would it be like to visualize that in a meditation? Buddhist believe that all human beings are born with the fullest of the Buddha nature within them. It only needs to be awakened.

Bob Proctor's statements, the Hindu, and Buddhist beliefs are much different from ancient Greek mythology. Zeus seemed to care little for humans but sired children everywhere and anywhere. Some of his children were misfits like the Vulcan god Hephystos. Hephystos suffered greatly in his body and in his soul because he was a shame to his godly parents. He was cast off Mount Olympus, the mountain of the gods, yet he was born of a god. I bring this example to light because Hephystos is an example of a human-god creation that from the beginning went array. While there are many myths as to the origin of Hephystos, in one of the myths, he was conceived through lust and held as a secret from Zeus' wife, Herra. A law of trust was broken. Hephystos was born a crippled god, his feet turned backward. The feet are all about one's direction in life. Hephystos suffered immensely before allowed to return to the mountain of the gods. He had to prove his godly powers. That is quite a task. If you take this seriously you are then implicitly invited to ask, what are your godly powers? Like Hephystos many humans are cast out of their families? Many people struggle to prove themselves to society, church, and family? This is a sad and unfortunate myth.

But the myth of "The Soul" is that there is only one soul to which we all belong. We are not born to live in competition. Rather, we belong to harmony and all the virtues that living a shared life affirms. If you can capture the myth of "The Soul," you will begin to realize what your godly responsibilities and powers are.

The stories of the Greek gods reflect to us over and over again both the blessings and the short sightedness of human beings and point out our own human frailties. The gods are powers indeed, but the myths about the gods reflect back to us just how foolish humans have been and continue to be. They also acknowledge the joys and tragedies of life. One must question if living a life of tragedies is necessary unless we can make meaning of them. In the Buddhist, Hindu and Native American beliefs there are laws of karma that govern why things happen. But these religions also believe that negative karma often can be avoided if one lives by the virtues of compassion, generosity, harmony, and love. Ekhart Tolle notes in his book *The Power of Now; A Guide to Spiritual Enlightenment*, "All the things that truly matter—beauty, love, creativity, joy, inner peace—arise from beyond the mind" (p. 14). The mind, in this case, is the frightened ego that wants to be in charge. But if we can put the ego aside and practice the virtues we awaken to a higher consciousness. Higher consciousness affirms that we all come from one Source, The Mind of Pure Light, and are intimately united. That is the world we return to when we die.

The Source

Perhaps you might ask, what is the Source from which we come? According to the mystics, the Source is light. Going back to the quantum physics theory, everything is made of light. From the believer's point of view, The Divine is Light, and that Light permeates every living and material thing. We are made of light, and that which is Divine is in us. We are made of a tiny part of the substance of Infinite Light. Hence one can affirm the mantra, "God and I are One." That is the first universal law. Yet, the Divine is beyond all thought, and therefore beyond all judgments. Divinity is beyond all form and therefore beyond all materiality, but at the same time permeates all that is. That is why Rumi says:

"You are not a drop in the ocean. You are the entire ocean in a drop." Rumi

In other words, Rumi encourages us to get in touch with the totality of Divinity contained within the soul. Rumi is saying that we belong to infinity. We do not believe it because our minds want to be in control. Yet in our very substance we are attached to Infinite Substance. Our experience of what is Divinity or Infinity is a WE experience because all of us have it. It is not possible to be an infinite entity all by one's self because all that has been created is made of the same Infinite Light. It is the mind or ego that wants to separate us from one another. The infinite union that we have with the Divine in death is also here now in life, while in a physical body. In essence all are united in one Soul. We are all made of the same Light. That is abundance. The good that happens for one person or being happens for them all. We are interconnected.

In many world religions, the Divine creates all that is, leaving light in all that is. Divinity is made of nonmaterial Light. All that is in the material world however is made from a visible entity called light. The material world is light condensed. The light that we are made from has been condensed from the invisible Light, or God. This invisible Light is what the Divine is made of. Hence, the Source of creation is within you, therefore, by your very nature you are intimately connected to the

Divine and like the Divine, you are a creative being. This is what it means to be a son or daughter of the Divine. We are creators like the Divine, or more appropriately put, we co-create with Divinity. Hence there is a phrase in the Gospel of John which states, "you are gods." Do you believe that? It is a remarkably high state of being, yet that is what we are. You were born to be creative and to experience abundance in its fullness. Abundance does not promise wealth, but that we will be provided for. It promises fullness and joy. The Dalai Lama says, "Your duty in life is to be happy." What is your happiness?

Chinguetti

Abundance comes in many ways. There is a New Atlantis Full Documentaries film called "Desert Gathering." It is about the Arabic Tuareg people who live in the desert on a last stronghold. Chinguetti is the seventh holy place of Islam. The under-riding theme of this movie is the struggle for survival in the face of what brings happiness. The desert is advancing on the city and available water decreasing. But while many families left the nomadic lifestyle, there are those who wish to stay and, if possible, remain in the desert. They desire to remain because the secrets of the nomadic life sustain them. Life in the desert is getting harder and more of their friends and relatives are leaving for other countries and city life.

In the film, a man who lives on the outskirts of Chinguetti with his camels and goats has tried city life but returned to the solace and power of desert living where peace still reigns, and family is the center and bond of living.

He says:

> At night, our parents used to stay up talking and singing until very late. My cousins, my brother and I would leave the palm grove and walk for a long time until the himas (tent lights) looked like small lightning bugs, and the canticles could barely be heard.
>
> Then, one day, because of the encroaching desert and the lure of changing times, everyone began to leave Chinguetti and its surrounding desert lands. One by one they left, and we never came together again. Chinguetti is the traditional, centuries old gathering place for our people and families.
>
> I've not gone to school, but I like to listen carefully to what people say. I've memorized a phrase that a foreigner once said to me. He said, 'Walking is in itself an encouraging movement. One's head becomes just as vivacious as one's legs. He who walks gives free reign to his fantasy, imagination, and thinking. He who walks this way has no possessions. Possessions require a sedentary life. You have to stay where you are. In the desert, nothing owns us, so we own everything.'"

(www.youtube.com/watch?v=8o2BLBuf6YA)

This man knows what it means to have a free spirit. He knows what happiness is for him. Freedom is his abundance, and he prefers the abundance of a more difficult life in the dessert than to live in the comforts of a large city.

The Saints

St. Francis of Assisi and Clare of Assisi (and many other saints) understood what being free of possessions was all about. Having taken the vow of poverty to its extreme, they lived lives of sheer abundance. If you trust in the Divine, you trust in yourself because you are a reflection of the Divine in the world. This is abundance.

At the same time, I have a number of friends who are very wealthy though none of their neighbors know it. They live modest lives in middle class neighborhoods. They are generous with their time and money. But they do not over give to their local church or town so as to be singled out as wealthy. I have had this discussion with some of my friends, and they prefer to be generous to outside agencies. They love their neighbors and church members and are highly active and of service. For them, they are blessed with wealth, but abundance to them is living and being with their neighborhood friends.

I have other friends who are also very wealthy and live in upscale neighborhoods. They and their children are some of the most humble, non-pretentious, welcoming, down to Earth people I've ever met. When we get together, we talk about themes that are written in this book. They value the interconnectedness of beings. They value harmonious living.

Harmony and Presence

If you hold harmony as a value, the likelihood is that you will be supported everywhere you go. The soul is intimately connected to this virtue. Harmony is not limited because it is a Divine aspect. You can be in harmony anywhere and everywhere and you can be at peace with all beings. This is the law of interconnection. Harmony is a state of mind that works through the heart. The state of presence brings about harmonious living. Harmony operates through active presence and therefore being in action. One has to be present to be One with all beings. One has to be present to be One with the Divine, as Divinity is in all things and beings. Presence is harmony. One cannot be harmonious without being present, because harmony works for the good of all beings, the good of all beings works in harmony with you. This is abundance.

True abundance begins with having a desire for the good of all beings.

Harmony is a moral state or place of being because it desires happiness for all. The state of harmony is active still presence. We become aware of this presence while active in the world. Even in meditation or with silent reflection, attentive presence has a very active component to it. This is because when the mind becomes still the soul is at work. Hence if we are aligned with our true service and calling, attentive presence will point us in the right direction. Even the right people will be brought our way.

There is no separation between your happiness and the happiness of other beings. Thus it follows, if you want happiness, then work for the happiness of other beings. Wherever you go, just be conscious of others and caring of and for them. Harmony then becomes the sharing of what one has with others as well as receiving from others what is needed. One has many gifts to share that go way beyond finances. There are many ways to be generous. If you truly love yourself, for example, you will live in harmony with all other beings. Harmony echoes the reassurance that there is one Source from which we all come. Source is our plenty, our abundance. When we step into that world of harmony, that world of being in a place of desiring for the good of all, we are in touch with Source. This is abundance.

Nothing is so divisive as the competitive mind, the unforgiving mind, the greedy mind, the angry mind, the selfish mind, or the controlling mind. None of these serve the higher Light.

When I finished writing the above paragraphs on harmony and presence, I was automatically taken into a meditative state and the following message came through:

> *All is well, all will be well as you are in this state. May the light shine through you for the good of all beings. There is hope now because you are present to what gives hope.*
>
> *At this moment in time there is an awakening calling that will assure you of the Now. It will work through you and transform both you and the world around if you allow it, if you let it. For you have been revealed, and a key has been revealed to you. You are forever changed by knowing this above teaching on harmony and have displayed how it flows into the other gifts, the other virtues. It is key to your future and the future of others. It is your abundance. If you can focus on abundance with this new understanding it will go well for you. There is more to come. There is always more to come.*

> *Essence is the place of being that allows for the presence of God. Where you live in Essence is your home. Essence is that connection to Source, from which you came. It is the care of you and of all beings. Essence is a state of being, a place of hope because it reveals God, the Source of being and therefore of hope.*

I chose to leave this quote in the text because it may help the reader as it inspires me.

The Soul and Financial Concerns

The soul wants to supply our needs and will take the lead to supply them if we have a goal and a life with soul. We may not become millionaires, as that goal may not be the soul's goal for us. However, as much as the soul leads us, we need to direct the soul. We need to inform it when our finances are low. Currently I have friends who have purchased homes that are quite large. They have wedded themselves deeply to financial commitments to the degree that if one of them gets ill or loses a job they will lose their house. Over-spending is never wise, and the soul does not support our hopes to have an image current with conventionalism. I have friends who have a beautiful house, all the right furniture, clothes and cars. But they have a great burden keeping up with the status image of the neighbors.

There are consequences for living such a lifestyle. First, the soul suffers. My friends are always worried about finances. Secondly, their children have become materialistic, but at the same time feel their parents worry. Two of their children resent their parents because they cannot have what their friends have. There is nothing wrong with having material things. But if we are attached to material things more than to what really matters in life, then we are remiss. Attachment to money and things is not happiness. But living safely and comfortably, and by that I mean having our needs met, is happiness. Happiness is what really matters.

To the degree that we nurture the soul it is free to grow. The soul does not need the material world, yet it is at work within it. The need for money is not part of its need. The angels, for instance, do not have a money system that they use for anything. Yet, they supply us with our daily needs, including the financial means to support ourselves. But because money is not part of their daily energy exchange system, they need to be reminded regularly to provide for us. There are times people are provided for and yet, money is not exchanged through their hands. The angels often work that way.

I recently met a man whom I will call Charles. Charles said he had a profound experience just the week before that he wanted to share. His sister called and asked him to pick up her son at college, as there was no one who could do it and Charlie lived only a couple of miles from the college. This was unusual as Charlie's sister rarely called upon him. When he went to pick up his nephew, he found him in tears. Charles asked what was going on. His nephew reported that he was just informed that he was behind in his tuition payments and therefore could not return to classes next semester. Uncle Charles went immediately to the finance office with his nephew to find that the bill owed was $100. Charles paid the bill and placed a $100 deposit fee for the next semester for his nephew. The nephew was again in tears, but this time elated and very happy. When he asked his uncle how he could do this for him so easily. Charlie told his nephew that he always loved him and always would.

In this story, the nephew never felt the money in his own hands, yet money was given to fulfill his need. It was a transaction that was done and completed before his eyes but never passed through his own hands. I learned that the nephew worked at a pizza parlor and did not have another source of income to support his college education. Uncle Charlie told me that it was a great joy for him to give $200 for his nephew. He believes that his nephew is trying hard to make ends meet, and he will help him again.

This story is an example of how the angels work behind the scenes. For nephew to experience the fulfillment of his need, not only did Charlie need to be put in his nephew's path, but Charlie was as much affected by his act of generosity as the student was by Charlie's generosity. Charlie was put in his nephew's path at a time when nephew was in great need. In fact, nephew was broken and sorrowful. In the moment of their meeting, Charlie needed to have a generous attitude for the miracle to happen. The angels orchestrated all of this for nephew. A question for us is, if someone is in need will we be available to assist? Generosity is a virtue that has to be cultivated. The need can take any shape or form, from giving a ride, to carrying an object for someone who cannot carry it, to giving finances to someone in need. Or, just being there with a friend. All are forms of generosity.

Spiritual Abundance

This section is for those who are asking deeper questions about their spiritual lives. Some people find that a spiritual path is their only path. There are many ways to walk that spiritual path. Some people on the planet know what it means to carry a burden for another. As a hospice chaplain, I see it all the time. Family members and neighbors come together to care for a dying patient. They see it as an act of gratitude. They are grateful to be able to do this difficult work for their family member or neighbor and see it as a blessing. I see families work together to pick up each other's children at school while another works. Grandmothers oversee their grandchildren while the parents are working. These are normal sacrifices that at the end of the day manifest as true signs of abundance. Abundance is with us everywhere.

I lived in the south side of Chicago from June 1985 to May 1987. This is an area of diversity and poverty. It was an area overseen by gangs. The religious brothers, priests, and nuns were the only white people living in that area. But everyone knew who we were, and most people respected and protected us.

One day a woman came to the rectory with a story to tell. Aretha had not had food for three days but was excited to tell her story before she even bought food for herself. She shared her story with Brother Steve. The woman was poor but very prayerful. She did not know her neighbors but often prayed for them. She had been asking God how she who had so little money would be able to help someone in need in her neighborhood. She explained with tears in her eyes to Brother Steve that her prayer was answered. She said she was full of joy because three days ago a woman with two children knocked on her door, and the mother informed her that they had absolutely nothing in their house to eat. The woman said she gave what she had. All she had was a jar of peanut butter and a loaf of bread. She said that it meant so much to her that she could give what she had away. She exclaimed, "I sat up in prayer and praise half the night for joy. Those children needed to eat, and their mother needed nourishment to look after them. All I had to do was get through two days without food and my social security check would come on the third day." It was the third day and Aretha had not yet eaten but had her check in hand. She was on her way to the bank to cash it and then to the grocery to satisfy her hunger. But for sheer joy, she came first to the rectory to share her story with Brother Steve.

This is a story of abundance experienced through trust in the Divine. These types of stories happen all the time, but few people hear them. Many saints throughout the ages knew of this abundance. Francis and Clare of Assisi and Mother Teresa are a few examples of trust that leads to abundance. Many people live spiritually abundant lives on this planet. They have all they want and all they need. They live day to day. I share these thoughts because there might be something we can learn about abundance for ourselves through study of other people's lives and acts of faith.

The opportunity to be of service is innate in everyone. It is part of our soul's identity. All of us participate in the service of others while simply meshing with human beings. At the same time, all of us are in need of service as well as have the need to serve. To be human is to be compassionate. Our planet has become one world. What we do and say and how we treat each other in the workplace, or the marketplace, etc., is significant! Our world is inter-connected, inter-faith, and cross-cultural. Yet, we are one people. To the extent that each human being accepts this in the heart, there will be either various levels of peace and unity, or various levels of division and war on this planet.

The question then comes down to the individual person. What are you creating? If you create nothing, you have buried your treasure and no result will come of it. If there is no sharing no one benefits. The buried treasure will be there waiting for you when you die with no merit to show for your tasks while on earth. If there are such things as karma and reincarnation, one is left with the question, "Do you really want to do this all over again?" Rather, it is better to move on with the life that was intended for you to live so you can ascend higher on the spiritual spiral and ladder.

As noted above, there is more to abundance than just becoming wealthy. Have you ever wondered what you might become if you are your very best, the very best and highest you? What would that look like? I suggest that you take a few minutes to go into meditation and visualize what the highest and best you might look like. Then, take a few minutes to visualize what the highest and best you might look like from the perspective of Divinity. What does that look like?

But how does one live their highest best in the tangible world? To learn this, you may need to ask your soul, what is my true "soul life purpose"? It is a law that if you seek to perform your true highest purpose, which can be called your "soul life purpose", you will be protected. You will not be invincible but protected. You will still suffer the human condition. But to perform your soul life purpose means you are drawing to yourself the heavenly helpers. We all have them, and they show up when we show up to them.

Summary Questions: Thoughts to Ponder Abundance As a Spiritual Process

1) Is what you desire to achieve the will of the Divine

for you? Or is what you desire what you yourself, your parents, or society expects from, or desires for you?

2) What is your premise? Mine is (hopefully, most of the time) to perform my true-life calling and purpose. I try to do that. It is a commitment.

3) Have you thought of having a good spiritual reading so you can learn what is your

    a. Soul Life Blue Print? (numerology—Wilhelm Oosthuizen or Robert Lee Camp)

    b. Your Horoscope (an astrology reading by Lynn Bell, Donna Steele, or Susan Chapman)

    c. Your Soul Life Colors, (Laura Alden Kamm)

    d. Learn what is your life song (the Masters and White Eagle)

    e. Your Invisible Garment (Connie Kaplan)

I would recommend a reading with anyone of the above-mentioned spiritual artists, and there are many more like them. Quality wholesome mediums are hard to find but they are out there.

4) Eben Pagan, Bob Proctor, and Mary Morrissey report that 80% of those who try to begin a new career fail. Is this because they are not working on their spiritual life purpose? Is it because they do not know how to apply spiritual principles to physical manifestation? The first principle of abundance is to realize that you are meant to manifest the virtues. The virtues are one of your direct connections to the soul. Meditation, prayer, spiritual presence, and homage are also connections to the soul. Even basic appreciation for all that we have and are given each day is a connection to the soul.

5) Beginning a new career can be hard work, yet most people will be called to a new career when they are in their forties, fifties, or sixties. Some people either

create or begin three or four new careers during their lives.

6) If you are meant to begin a new career you will find that you may need to learn new talents and skills. You may have to go back to school to get a degree.

7) You will not be able to bring in the new unless you have processed and let go of the old. This is hard work and one must be diligent about it for a while before the letting go process happens. Such a process may demand the help of a Spiritual Director, Therapist, or Life Coach. Once you are free of the trappings of the past you will receive a calling to move forward with the career of your Soul Life Blueprint. Your Soul Life Blueprint is the map of what you came here on planet Earth to do.

8) Some questions to ask yourself when beginning a new career are: Is your goal realistic? Are you looking at building a viable business? Is the business you are creating needed and sought after by the public?

   a. Are you presently living beyond your means? Then you need to learn what that is all about before you begin a new business venture.

   b. Are you presently living under your means? Then you will need to look at what that is all about before you begin a new business venture.

   c. Why do you need a change in profession? Have you clearly identified the reasons? If you have identified the reasons for a change of profession, what holds you back?

9) We have to be willing to look at the fact that the business world has changed and is in the process of changing again and quite rapidly. There is more competition and more money consciousness in the world of business. At the same time, there appears to be less concern by corporations for the people who use

their products or the people who make them. It might be important for you to be aware of the moral codes that you operate out of?

10) We need to learn new business skills to navigate on this planet. This means that we need to learn the appropriate new technologies that accompany our times.

11) Many people find that they are spiritually and emotionally challenged by the values of the consumer world. Consumer industries are not easy places for a sensitive person to work in. That alone has become a leading reason for people wanting to begin their own business.

12) So, the question comes back to you, why are you leaving your job (or wanting to leave your job)? Articulating your experience is important.

a. Some people leave their jobs because they believe they have been mistreated.

b. Is it too stressful – name the stresses, what are they?

c. People feel misunderstood...

d. ...Because burnout happens when we do much of the same thing at work or at home for too long a period of time, it may be called workaholism.

e. ...Or, perhaps you have the desire for financial freedom.

f. Many people feel little or no gratification in their current job.

13) What price are you willing to pay for peace of mind and peace in your body?

Personal success only happens when you do your personal internal work, meaning how deep you have gone into the soul. We go into the soul when we ask the above and other questions. To the degree that you have done your internal work measures how much your gifts and talents will be able to influence the world about you. Very often internal work shows that you are willing to work physically as well. This book was written after my work hours and on weekends over a period of three years. It was required of me to write this book. It was a sacrifice that demanded I let go of all the extras to become what matters for others. This book is an abundance as seen from the eyes of Spirit. I have gained much from writing this book. The abundance continues if people engage with what is written here.

It would be the same if you were to start your own business. There are different types of aspirations that one may have to begin a business. All of them will be shaped by the fact that we live on this earth and must conform to the spiritual and temporal laws that govern our environment. Mother Teresa started an organization that spread to the world. Her organization is also a business. Like everything else on the planet Mother Teresa's order is run by money and has an administrator. But behind all of that is an aspiration and, I am sure, lots of prayer.

14) If you desire to create a new career you would do well to study the nature of Quantum physics. Any new career requires a quantum leap.

15) The purpose for you being here on planet Earth is because you have a gift and that gift needs to be offered or manifested in the world. We are all born with a specific unique gift that needs to be expressed. You are the gift. So what one needs to do is find out what the gift is and then get out of the way. This means you have work to do. First you must discover what your gift is. Be educated to or about that gift and what it needs. That gift is the work that you need to do while on this planet.

What is your gift?

16) When you begin any profession or company, always remember that soul is not a singular experience but a collective experience. We all come from the same source, from a collective soul. Therefore, working with the spiritual laws is a good place to start any endeavor.

Suggested Readings

Dalai Lama and Jeffrey Hopkins. *Mind of Clear Light: Advice on Dying and Living a Better Life*. New York; Atria Books. 2002.

Dalai Lama and Jeffrey Hopkins. *How to Practice: The Way to a Meaningful Life*. New York; Pocket Books. 2002.

Brown, Dee. *Bury My Heart at Wounded Knee: An Indian History of the American West*. New York; Open Road, 1970.

Jung, Carl G. *Modern Man in Search of a Soul*. New York; Harvest. 1933.

Jung, Carl G. *Psychology and Religion: West and East*. Carl G. New Jersey; Princeton University Press. 1969.

Jung Carl. G. *The Symbolic Life*. New Jersey; Princeton University Press. 1977.

Kahlil Gibran. *The Prophet*. New Your; Alfred A Knopf, Inc. 1979.

Karmapa, Ogyen Trinley Dorge. *Interconnected: Embracing Life in Our Global Society*. Somerville, MA; Wisdom Publications. 2017.

Kingsley, Peter. *A Story Waiting to Pierce You: Mongolia, Tibet and the Destiny of the Western World*. Point Reyes, CA; The Golden Sufi Center. 2010.

Neihardt, John G. *Black Elk Speaks*. Lincoln; University of Nebraska Press. 1961.

Tolle, Eckhart. *The Power of Now: A Guide to Spiritual Enlightenment*. Vancouver; Namaste Publishing. 1997.

Price Pritchett. *You2: A High-Velocity Formula for Multiplying Your Personal Effectiveness in*

Quantum Leaps. Dallas; Pritchett and Associates. 2012.

About the Author

Gary German's life is led by a deep sense of having a calling. At age 22, he left the family farm in Nebraska to pursue the life of a Franciscan priest. As a student of theology Gary was drawn to experience life with the Lakota Sioux in South Dakota. Profound experiences with Indigenous Americans have greatly changed his world view. As a Catholic priest Gary ministered in areas of Diversity in Chicago; with Latino American populations in South Texas, and with Native Americans in New Mexico. Throughout this time his experience grew broad and deep which guided him to study 13 different religions and their accompanying cultures resulting in a doctoral degree; Mythological Studies, Emphasis Depth Psychology. In 2000 Gary left clerical ministry to become an inter-faith chaplain. Currently, Gary continues as a Spiritual Counselor. As a hospice chaplain he meets regularly with patients and their families, runs groups for the bereaved, and offers counseling to nurses and families deeply impacted by COVID-19.

Gary remains a spiritual director and guide for those seeking a journey with the soul. For further inquiry you may check out his website at walkingsoulfully.com

www.ingramcontent.com/pod-product-compliance
Lightning Source LLC
Chambersburg PA
CBHW061431040426
42450CB00007B/993